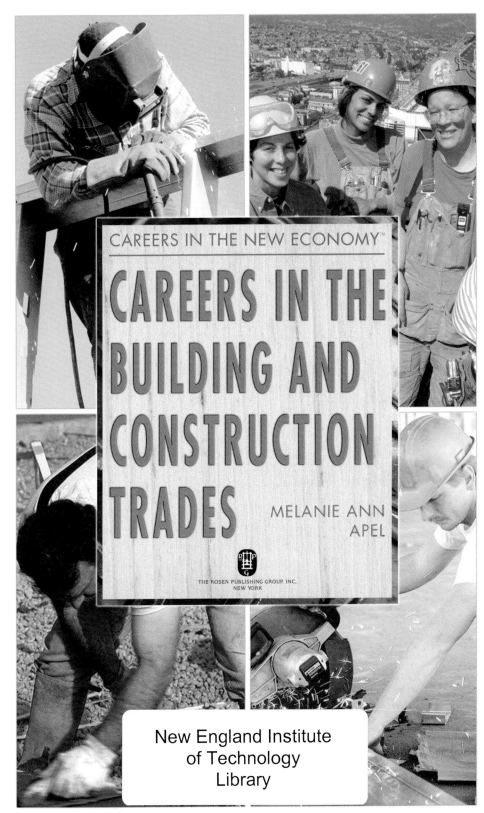

CAREERS IN THE NEW ECONOMY™

CAREERS IN THE BUILDING AND CONSTRUCTION TRADES

MELANIE ANN
APEL

THE ROSEN PUBLISHING GROUP, INC.
NEW YORK

For Hayden, of course! Love, Mommy

Published in 2005 by The Rosen Publishing Group, Inc.
29 East 21st Street, New York, NY 10010

Library of Congress Cataloging-in-Publication Data

Apel, Melanie Ann.
Careers in the building and construction trades/Melanie Ann Apel.—1st ed.
    p. cm.—(Careers in the new economy)
Includes bibliographical references and index.
ISBN 1-4042-0251-X (library binding)
1. Building trades—Vocational guidance—United States. 2. Construction industry—Vocational guidance—United States.
I. Title. II. Series.
HD9715.U52A85 2005
624'.023'73—dc22

2004008427

Manufactured in the United States of America

Photo credits: Cover, pp. 1 (top left and bottom left and right), 3 (first, second, and fourth from top), 4–5, 7, 25, 71, 92, 107, 111, 133, 138, 140 © Nova Department Corporation; cover (middle inset), pp. 1 (top right), 3 (third from top), 51 © AP/Wide World Photos; p. 10 courtesy Eddy Wright/ Bolingbrook, IL; pp. 14, 28, 34–35, 41 © *Electrican's Exam Preparation Guide*, 5th Edition, by John E. Trister/Revised and updated by Dale C. Bricker/Carlsbad, CA: Craftsman Book Company (1-800-829-8123 or http://www.craftsman-book.com), 2002, 7th printing; p. 27 chart reprinted with permission from the National Joint Apprenticeship and Training Committee (http://www.njatc.org); p. 48 © http://www.electrician.com; pp. 54, 55, 59 © *Plumber's Exam Preparation Guide* by Howard C. Massey/ Carlsbad, CA: Craftsman Book Company (1-800-829-8123 or http://www. craftsman-book.com), 2002, 7th printing; p. 61 © Louis J. Mahieu, *The Plumber's Toolbox Manual*/Arco Books, NY: Macmillan General Reference, 1989.

Designer: Nelson Sá; **Editor:** Kathy Kuhtz Campbell;
Photo Researcher: Nelson Sá

CONTENTS

INTRODUCTION

I t is not uncommon for a young person to come across a construction site and watch the machines haul large pieces of lumber and workers craft walls and building facades by hand using bricks and mortar. Perhaps that young person thought, "Wow, that looks like fun!" Who would not be amazed when watching a virtual pile of rubble turn into an actual office building or a home? Perhaps you have watched a building go up near your own home and you have thought about how exciting it would be to take part in such a remarkable work in progress. Maybe you have even said to yourself, "I think I would like to work in construction."

If you choose a career in carpentry, electricity, masonry, plumbing, or tiling, you will master a skill that will carry you through your lifetime. You will be employable until you are ready to retire. After all, homes, buildings, garages, and other structures are always being built, and people are constantly remodeling and renovating existing homes, offices, and all sorts of other buildings. Where there are people, there is always a need for shelter and waste management systems (in other words, homes and bathrooms). While many businesses in today's economy are feeling the pressure of hard times, it is quite apparent when you walk through many urban and suburban neighborhoods that the building and construction industry is booming. Things are looking good for the future of the building and construction industry.

According to a January 2004 article in *Plumbing and Mechanical Magazine*, employment in the construction industry was still on the rise after ten months and was so good it broke a record set almost two years before. Between February and December 2003, the construction industry had increased employment with 173,000 jobs. This gain was in contrast with jobs in other fields, of which 285,000 jobs were terminated. The article goes on to say that "over the past year, employment has risen by approximately 17,000 in construction of buildings, 4,000 in heavy and civil engineering construction, and 5,000 among specialty trade contractors." The pay salaries were looking good as well. The average hourly wage of a construction worker in 2003 saw a 29¢ increase over the year, bringing the average hourly wage to $19.10 and the average weekly wage to $723.09 based on an average workweek consisting of just less than thirty-eight hours.

Depending on the area in which you are planning to work, and depending on the needs of the town or city, you may find more construction projects or fewer. Although fluctuation from year to year is certain, it may be safe to say that when it comes to construction in general, if you are educated, skilled, licensed, and ready to work, it will not be too hard to find a job that will allow you an ample income.

Each of the trades you will read about in this book—carpentry, electricity, plumbing, masonry, and tiling—often require you to complete an apprenticeship, including a certain number of on-the-job training hours before you can begin your career.

An apprenticeship is a system of teaching and learning in which a person who wishes to learn a trade works under the close supervision of an employer who teaches him or her the skills and provides him or her with the knowledge to become proficient in a chosen trade. The apprenticeship can be compared to schooling; when a person completes an apprenticeship, he or she should be ready to enter the workforce. An apprentice, therefore, is someone who learns a trade or art by gaining experience while working under the supervision of a skilled worker. An apprenticeship may last from two to five years, depending on one's prior experience and the number of hours required by the particular trade. Most apprenticeships are combined with classroom instruction. Within each chapter and in the For More Information section of this book, you will learn more about the apprenticeships of the individual trades and where to go for additional information on becoming an apprentice.

There are many career opportunities available to someone looking into the field of building and construction for employment. Not only are there many different types of jobs, but there are various work conditions, too. For example, tradespeople may find jobs with large corporations or large construction firms. They may decide to join a building maintenance team. Or they may want to venture out to owning companies of their own, becoming individual contractors or the sole proprietors. Their businesses may be specialized or they may be general, and they may be the owners and workers or they may have teams of employees who work in one or many trades.

CHAPTER 1

CARPENTER

A carpenter is a worker who builds or repairs things made of wood. The word "carpentry" refers to the building of structures. Carpentry is often confused with another similar-sounding career field: cabinetry. But cabinetry is, as its name implies, the building of cabinets and furniture in general, and carpentry involves the building of larger structures such as sheds, staircases, and houses.

In the words of carpenter Jacob Fisher of Philadelphia, Pennsylvania, "Carpentry is the art of combining rough and finish materials with high- and low-tech tools, to create shelter and sanctuary."

The field of carpentry can actually be divided into two parts: structural carpentry and finishing carpentry. A structural carpenter builds the framework of a structure. Then, the finishing carpenter takes over. He or she adds the finishing touches, such as installing the molding and ceiling and wall panels, hanging doors and windows, and installing trim inside the new structure.

A WORKING CARPENTER'S VIEWPOINT

Jacob Fisher of Philadelphia is a carpenter. He describes his work as follows:

> *My job title is sole proprietor, which means I am self-employed, with my own business, and I have two men who work with me full-time. I am a master carpenter, working exclusively in residential renovations. I primarily design and build projects. My primary responsibilities are responding to and creating relationships with my clients and the people who work with me, and then creating and producing the projects they want. My secondary responsibilities, then, are as manager, designer, and salesperson, and I also have to make estimates, train my employees, and make sawdust! What I am creating is a business that provides the space for other craftsmen to express themselves and for my clients to see their dreams fulfilled.*

WHAT A CARPENTER DOES

If you choose a career in carpentry, you will have the opportunity to work on all sorts of different construction jobs. The actual tasks of a carpenter will depend on the nature of the job he or she is currently working on. The individual employer will determine exactly what work is to be done by the carpenter. According to the U.S. Department of Labor, carpenters "cut, fit, and assemble wood and other materials for the construction of buildings, highways, bridges, docks, industrial plants, boats, ships, and many other structures." They also build ventilation walls and partitions, called brattices, which are located in underground passageways. Brattices control air circulation in the passageways for other workers. Carpenters often specialize in a few specific tasks, such as erecting scaffolding, installing interior or exterior trim, or setting forms for concrete construction.

Carpenters with these areas of specialization are more likely to find employment with specialty trade contractors, who are hired by builders. But if the middleman—a specialty trade contractor—is skipped and the carpenter is working directly for the general building contractor, it will more than likely be necessary for him or her to have a wide range of skills in order to perform tasks such as installing doors and windows, laying hardwood floors, building stairs, framing walls and partitions, and hanging kitchen cabinets.

An employable carpenter will know the local building codes for the city and state in which that carpenter works, which often specify exactly where and how certain carpentry materials can and cannot be used. One such building code, for example, is that "any wood coming in contact with concrete must be pressure treated," explains carpenter Eddy Wright of Bolingbrook, Illinois, because concrete tends to trap moisture and will cause untreated wood to rot. Building codes are important regulations for the carpenter to be aware of before he or she starts any job.

While no two carpentry jobs will be exactly the same, a carpenter follows the same basic steps for most jobs.

THE CARPENTER AT WORK

When beginning a new job, the carpenter will start with either instructions from the supervisor or a blueprint. First, the carpenter will create a layout from these specifications. He or she measures, marks, cuts, shapes, levels, and arranges the materials for the job. Then, using power tools or hand tools (or a combination of both), such as chisels, drills, planes, sanders, and saws, the carpenter will cut the materials and get them into the proper shape. The materials a carpenter works with include drywall, fiberglass, insulation, plastic, plywood, wallboard, and wood.

Next, the carpenter will use adhesives, nails, screws, or staples to join the materials together. To finish the work, the carpenter has to check everything he or she has done to make sure the work is accurate. He or she will use framing squares, levels, plumb bobs, and tape measures to check for accuracy. If any inaccuracies are found, the carpenter will make any adjustments to remedy the inaccuracy.

The carpenter's job is made simpler if he or she works on jobs that use prefabricated materials, such as wall panels or stairs. Prefabricated materials are made to be installed quickly and easily, usually in one operation. The prefabricated materials are made with fewer pieces that need to be cut or assembled, or even laid out.

Some carpenters remodel homes or similar buildings. These carpenters have to be skilled at all aspects of a job rather than specializing in one or two types of tasks. This is why you will be doing yourself a favor by getting as

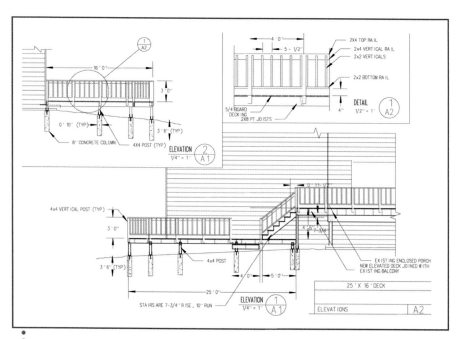

A carpenter's blueprint shows the elevation and construction details of a plan for building a deck measuring 25 feet by 16 feet (7.6 meters by 4.9 meters) onto a house. The drawing at the top left depicts the side elevation of the deck. The top right drawing shows a detailed plan of the circled portion of the rail in that side elevation view.

much training in as many different areas of carpentry as possible. With a broader repertoire of skills, you will be more easily employed because you will have the means to work on remodeling jobs, residential buildings, and commercial construction projects alike.

A FUTURE IN SAWDUST: THE OUTLOOK FOR A CAREER IN CARPENTRY

If you decide to go forward with your plans to become a carpenter, you are heading in a good direction. Employment opportunities for carpenters are excellent and should continue to be so until at least the year 2010. The main reason for the large number of expected job openings is the great number of carpenters who are likely to retire from the trade in upcoming years. In addition to the retirees, others are leaving because, according to carpenter Chris Sainz of Lake-in-the-Hills, Illinois, "many people with limited skills take jobs as carpenters but eventually leave the occupation because they dislike the work or cannot find steady employment," since there are "no strict training requirements for entry." Thus, anyone who has taken the time to become properly trained for this career will be in great shape for taking advantage of those opportunities.

Job opportunities for carpenters are not expected to increase as quickly as job opportunities in other trades. However, job opportunities are still expected to increase. Demand for more and more homes, office buildings, and industrial and commercial plants not only to be built but also to be renovated will continue to increase, thereby creating more jobs. Wealthier families are building new homes as well as second, or vacation, homes. The increase in the immigrant population who might have more limited financial means brings carpenters to the task of installing smaller manufactured housing, starter homes, and rental apartments. On the downside, fewer carpenters will be needed for tasks that can now be done by machine, such as roof assemblies that can be lifted to the tops of houses by cranes. In addition, many building components, such as walls and stairs, are being prefabricated, and better adhesives decrease joining and drying times. The work of the carpenter is more efficient today than in years past.

Like many of the occupations in the building and construction industry, most of the work depends on a number of variable factors. You will find that most carpentry jobs offer only short-term employment due to the "cyclical nature of the construction industry," says Chris Sainz, as well as fluctuating interest rates, availability of mortgage funds, government spending, and business investment. In other words, when times are tough, when the economy is poor, people do not build as much as they do when the economy is looking good. In addition, you may find that carpentry is also a seasonal job. The part of the country in which you live and work has a lot to do with how many jobs there are because of the nature of the weather in a particular area. Local economic status, number of businesses, and overall population will also dictate the number of employment opportunities in a given area.

Because there have been so many innovations in tools, equipment, materials, and techniques, as well as new improvements to those already in existence, today's carpenter is more versatile than ever. So a carpenter who has well-rounded skills and abilities will find it much easier to gain employment than one who is limited in what he or she knows how to do. Some of the specialties you may aspire to within the carpentry trade include cabinetmaker, floor layer, interior systems carpenter, joiner, lather and drywaller, millwright, pile driver, and residential carpenter. The carpenters' union, the United Brotherhood of Carpenters and Joiners of America (UBC), offers apprenticeships in each of the carpentry specialties.

WAGES

According to Jacob Fisher, the annual salary range for carpentry is $45,000 and up. According to the May 2003 National Occupational Employment and Wage Estimates from the Bureau of Labor Statistics of the U.S. Department of Labor, hourly wages for a carpenter were reported at an average of $17.75 per hour in the year 2003. Even the low end of the hourly carpentry rate at roughly $10.04, which is earned by about 10 percent of all carpenters, is good. At the top 10 percent, a carpenter in 2003 was making $28.00 per hour. That comes to about $20,800 to $33,000 as a starting salary, an average salary of $36,920 per year, and up to $58,240 or more for a highly experienced carpenter. So, as you can see, the range is broad, but the average is definitely not bad at all. Of course, due to bad weather and bad economy and such, at times a carpenter will earn less than the average because there may not be as much work available.

THE WORK ENVIRONMENT

Jacob Fisher describes his typical work environment as "a challenging mix of dirt and debris, creating [most often] in an occupied and finished home, [where there is] limited space for materials, staging areas, and tools."

Carpentry can be, at times, a physically demanding occupation. You might find yourself bending, kneeling, or standing for long stretches of time. Your greatest risk of physical injury will be from the sharp and rough tools and materials that you will work with, as well as the power equipment you will use on the job. The other risk to your physical well-being is the possibility of falling while on the job, as you may be working at the top of a ladder or as high up as multiple stories, hanging from scaffolding. You may also feel uncomfortable working outside at times. Depending on where you live, you may find yourself working outdoors in the peak of summer, when the sun's midday rays are hottest. At other times, you may be working bundled against the chill of winter. A heavy downpour or thunderstorm may send you home for the day, but a passing spring shower is often endured. For these reasons, you will enjoy your work better and find yourself better prepared for your work environment if you take the time to prepare your body through exercise. A strong body makes for a well-equipped worker.

National Estimates for Carpenters as Reported in May 2003 by the U.S. Department of Labor, Bureau of Labor Statistics

Employment estimate and mean wage estimates for this occupation:

Employment (1)	Employment RSE (3)	Mean hourly wage	Mean annual wage (2)	Wage RSE (3)
852,080	1.0 %	$17.75	$36,920	0.4 %

Percentile wage estimates for carpenters:

Percentile	10%	25%	50% (Median)	75%	90%
Hourly Wage	$10.04	$12.66	$16.47	$21.85	$28.00
Annual Wage (2)	$20,890	$26,330	$34,250	$45,440	$58,240

1. Estimates for detailed occupations do not sum to the totals because the totals include occupations not shown separately. Estimates do not include self-employed workers.
2. Annual wages have been calculated by multiplying the hourly mean wage by a year-round, full-time hours figure of 2,080 hours.
3. The relative standard error (RSE) is a measure of the reliability of a survey statistic. The smaller the relative standard error, the more precise the estimate.

Two Carpenters Offer Their Insights About Their Careers

Eddy Wright: From Carpenter to Construction Superintendent

Eddy Wright of Bolingbrook, Illinois, held a construction superintendent position for many years. But he did not always hold such a prestigious position. Wright worked hard as a carpenter for a number of years, learning the ropes and honing his skills.

I started as a laborer, then I did rough carpentry (framing, building walls and roofs), and then finish carpentry (paneling, trim, doors, etc.) before, finally, I worked my way up to the construction superintendent position. I never went to school to learn carpentry and construction. Construction was my summer job while attending school. But technical or vocational schools can teach the basics. Construction management courses are available, too.

Most construction companies will take strong candidates and put them through an internship program—an assistant superintendent position for smaller jobs. You will learn to work with the trades [subcontractors], coordinating their activities and managing others to get the job done. For two years I worked as an assistant superintendent. This time was invaluable in gaining experience about construction management in the field.

The superintendent has overall on-site responsibility for the project. I was expected to ensure the job [was] completed not only on time but also under budget and at the level of quality that is expected by the client. I was primarily responsible for maintaining the job timeline, locating and contracting subcontractors, scheduling the contractors, handling inspections and local governments, and representing the construction company to the customer. In addition, I was responsible for general public relations with the city and with the public, as well as policing the activities of everyone working on the job site. Experience in construction is the key requirement for someone who wants to become a construction superintendent. Good organization and communication skills are important, as well as decision-making and people management—you are the boss after all. You need a strong personality to command the overall project. Important, and often not popular, decisions have to be made without 100 percent of the information needed. Flexibility is key as well, because travel is typically required with construction jobs.

When I started working, I made around $25,000 a year. I capped at around $40,000 a year when I left the field in 1993.

The work environment was diverse. New construction started as an empty lot and evolved into a building over ninety days. Remodels varied tremendously—sometimes it was a simple job like repainting a building, sometimes it was a major addition. My recommendation to anyone looking into this field of work as a career is this: Get experience in the field through the trades; carpentry is often the first place that superintendents get training. Attend vocational classes on construction management.

The future is bright for construction superintendents. Every construction job needs to be managed. Good superintendents will always be in demand.

CHRIS SAINZ, CARPENTER CONTRACTOR

Chris Sainz's brand-new business cards boldly advertise his new company. Sainz is a carpenter contractor, and as his business card notes, he will work on basements, kitchens, bathrooms, decks, and fences. But Chris did not always work for himself. The route to becoming a carpenter contractor was not an easy one.

My name is Chris Sainz. I'm twenty-four years old, and I live in Lake-in-the-Hills, Illinois. I am a carpenter. I'm also a carpenter contractor. The carpenter is the guy who does the work, and the contractor is the guy who gets the work for the carpenters to do. But right now I am wearing both hats. Building is my primary responsibility. Coordinating and estimating are my secondary responsibilities. I have to coordinate the trades on the bigger jobs. The plumbers, the electricians—all of their work has to coordinate with the work of the carpenter. I maintain the schedule for the work my men and I are doing. I estimate the jobs: how much money they will cost, how much time they will take. Then I do the actual carpentry as well. Today, I built a front porch and a door for a passageway between two houses here in the city. I build decks, remodel kitchens and bathrooms; I do windows, doors, fences. I build and fix these things.

It seems Chris was destined to become a carpenter.

I've been doing carpentry work since I was fourteen years old. I started out as a laborer. The laborer is the guy who picks up the scraps, hauls the materials, and takes away the garbage. Kind of like the bus boy of the carpentry trade. I did that for eight months. So after high school, I did a four-year apprenticeship to become a carpenter. The apprenticeship I did was through the District Council of Carpenters and Joiners. I went to the union hall and signed up. Then I waited for about six months to be called. I went to the Elk Grove Village campus. There are three others in Illinois. Then I was required to be in the classroom for one week every three months. During the rest of the time, I was learning on the job. To qualify for health-care benefits, you had to do 250 hours of work per quarter—so, per three months. During the apprenticeship, you learn how to use the tools; you learn to do the basic math. You learn layouts, how to do specific spacings of projects, such as walls.

You're learning . . . the building codes. There are different ones for different types of housing and for different areas in which you work. Then you do the hands-on building. We built small houses about half the size of a garage. Then we scrapped them. You are expected to be there on time and do your work every day.

I would say that a person thinking of becoming a carpenter has to be able to talk to people. And he has to be somewhat rigid. By that I mean that he has to be able to stand his ground and stay firm when quoting a price for a job. People will try to get you to give them a better price. But you know how much the job costs in terms of time, labor, and materials. So you can't back down on that. You also have to be good with your hands. You have to be able to think, especially mathematically. But there are tricks to everything. Lots of the tools of the trade have some of these tricks right on them. They all come with pamphlets to guide you through calculations, too. The thing is, when you are being paid to do a job, the customers want the job done quickly. They don't want you sitting down with a pencil and paper working out a calculation.

Now I am licensed under the union. It's not a personal license. I hold a membership card to the union. I have to buy a new one every three months. It costs $75 each time. When I go to a big job, a commercial job downtown, for example, I am required to show my union card. There's a job steward on the big jobs like that and he has to check our cards. But he has to show us his card first. I didn't have to show my card today because the job I did was residential.

And how is the pay?

A carpenter usually starts out at about $35,000 a year. We sign a contract every four years that guarantees us a raise that comes to about $2 an hour every year. A residential carpenter will make $50,000 to $55,000 a year. A *commercial carpenter will make $60,000 for a forty-hour workweek. Overtime will get you a salary of $80,000 a year. The residential carpenter can't make as much money because of the weather. When it's really bad out, you just don't work.*

My typical work environment is the great outdoors. When I am building a house, I show up and there's nothing there but the rough form, the concrete foundation. It's a big box; there's no ceiling, no walls, no real floor, just the concrete. We build the walls and the rooms, we cut [build] the roof and then put up the plywood. We lay the subfloor for the second floor. Today, I worked on an existing home where the owner needed a new front porch built at the top of the outdoor stairs. It was windy and cold out today. And, of course, I deal with being dirty a lot. In the summer, it can be very hot. Sometimes, especially when we are working on a brand-new house, there is nowhere to get warm or even [go to the] bathroom. That's where the port-o-johns come in handy. Of course, they aren't luxurious!

My advice to someone looking to get into this line of work is to learn everything you can. And be a little tough! The boss will yell at you a lot in the beginning. You have to get used to that. There is a magazine called Carpenter. The union puts it out every three months. It tells you all the who, what, and where of the industry. You can pick it up at any union hall. Just about every big city has its own union hall.

LOOKING FORWARD TO A LONG CAREER

If you decide to become a carpenter, you will be happy to know that just about every community throughout the United States employs carpenters. So, no matter where you live, chances are there will be work for you. Your employer may change from job to job, however. You may find yourself working exclusively for a contractor or exclusively as the contractor yourself, or you may alternate between the two.

In 2002, 1.2 million jobs were held by carpenters across the United States. This statistic put carpenters in the largest group of building trades that year. The U.S. Bureau of Labor Statistics breaks down this 1.2 million figure as follows:

- About 33 percent worked for general building contractors.
- About 20 percent worked for special trade contractors.
- About 12 percent worked in heavy construction.
- Most of the remaining 35 percent worked for manufacturing firms, government agencies, wholesale and retail establishments, and schools.

The Bureau of Labor Statistics also reports that 25 percent of the carpenters were self-employed.

As your career gains ground, you will happily find room for growth within the industry. Your opportunities come from the fact that you have gained experience working with the various materials and in all aspects of the industry and that you are familiar with all parts of the construction process, which will generally promote you into a position as a supervisor. You may become a general construction supervisor or a carpentry supervisor. Or you may become an independent contractor. The requirements for these positions are the ability to estimate what materials and how much of these materials will be needed to do the job, and to make accurate estimations about the amount of money it should take to complete a job, as well as how long it will take to complete it.

GETTING STARTED

So, now that you know the basics about a career in carpentry, you are ready to embark on this creative career path. How should you get started?

Most carpenters learn their trade from a combination of formal training and on-the-job training. You will undoubtedly learn a great deal just from being at work with professional carpenters and watching how they hone their craft. You may wish to enroll in a vocational school to learn the fine details of carpentry. Most likely, however, you will find yourself in an apprenticeship, or employer training program.

This last option, the apprenticeship, is the training path most often recommended by those who employ carpenters. You will be able to find an appropriate apprenticeship program by checking with the United Brotherhood of Carpenters and Joiners of America, the Associated General Contractors, Inc., or the National Association of Home Builders. Information on how to contact each of these organizations is listed in the back of this book. You may also find a training program through your local chapter of the Associated Builders and Contractors or your local Associated General Contractors, Inc., chapter. In these programs, you will find a combination of on-the-job training and classroom instruction related to your hands-on work.

While on the job as an apprentice, you will learn about elementary structural design. You will become familiar with common carpentry jobs, such as:

- **Form building:** This involves constructing a container to hold concrete while it is poured in place. The forms are typically made of wood and are leveled and braced to be as straight as possible. Sometimes steel is used to make forms. For example, to pour a sidewalk, you would need to place a form on each side, then place a string line down each inside top edge of the form to ensure that it is straight and level, then brace it with numerous stakes so that it won't move while the concrete is being poured.

- **Inside finishing:** Also known as finish carpentry, these are the finishes, such as hardwood trim and floors, paneling, window and door casings, paint, and wallpaper, that will be seen by the customer.

- **Layout:** This involves laying out the walls according to the floor plan, in other words, determining where the walls should go and marking out guidelines for the studs.
- **Outside finishing:** This is the same as inside finishing except it is seen on the outside of the building. It includes siding, soffits, fascia, trim, window and door casings, as well as brick and paint.
- **Rough framing:** This involves the parts of the walls and ceiling that are not seen by the naked eye, such as the wall studs, floor joists, and trusses. Rough framing is known as the internal skeleton of a house that is being built.

You will also learn how to use the various carpentry tools, machines, equipment, and materials. In addition, you will learn basic mathematics, how to read a blueprint, the various techniques of carpentry, and how to make freehand sketches.

Moreover, you will learn the basics of how carpentry is not just an isolated trade but a trade that relates to the various other building trades. For example, the carpenter and the electrician must work together to be sure that the components of their work meet each other's requirements. If the electrician is planning to install an electrical outlet in a certain spot, for instance, the carpenter might want to know ahead of time where to leave space for the outlet. You will also be taught the important fundamentals of job safety and first aid. The Occupational Safety and Health Administration (OSHA) of the U.S. Department of Labor works to ensure the safety and health of America's workers by setting and enforcing standards and by providing a training program in workplace safety. People can become OSHA certified in their trades after completing the safety training. See OSHA's Web site for additional information, http://www.osha.gov.

BECOMING AN APPRENTICE

To become a carpenter apprentice, you will have to meet several requirements. Most carpentry apprenticeships require that you be at least seventeen years old. A high school diploma, while especially helpful, is not a requirement. However, it is always beneficial to have a high school diploma in any venture you may consider. While you are still in high school, you should consider taking courses that will help you with your future carpentry career. You will do well to take classes in subjects such as carpentry, English, general mathematics, mechanical drawing, and shop.

In addition to the things you will learn in high school, you will want to bring certain personal traits to your career. You should have the following physical traits to be a good carpenter: you should be physically fit, have an excellent sense of balance, have strong eye-hand coordination, and have good manual dexterity.

Also to your advantage on the job will be the ability to solve arithmetic problems accurately and quickly. You will also find yourself at an advantage with employers if you have any work experience and/or training from the armed forces or Job Corps. Job Corps is a U.S. Department of Labor program that offers students from ages sixteen to twenty-four basic education and vocational training.

In addition to the age requirement and the physical preferences, you will have to meet certain local requirements to enter an apprenticeship. Some local unions may ask you to take a test of your aptitude for carpentry, for example. This is an important test to determine how long your apprenticeship will last. Depending on your aptitude and the skill level you bring to your apprenticeship, you can expect your program to last from approximately three to four years.

Unlike the availability of carpentry positions nationwide, carpentry apprenticeships are often hard to come across. So, for this particular trade, you do not have to rely on an apprenticeship to get a job. You are more likely to find yourself learning the skills you need while doing some informal on-the-job training. Of course, this type of training will not be as detailed or as rigorous as an apprenticeship would be. If you are interested in learning a wider variety of skills, you will do best to get your on-the-job training with a large general contractor rather than with a small contractor, who may teach you only one or two rough skills. You may eventually decide that you wish to specialize your carpentry skills into one specific area of work. However, when you are just starting out, it will be to your benefit to learn as many skills in as wide a variety of types of carpentry as possible. This gives you the flexibility to do just about anything, and therefore you will be more likely to find employment.

Once you have become a carpenter, you may consider joining the United Brotherhood of Carpenters and Joiners of America. Nearly 125 years old, the UBC was formed in 1881 by thirty-six carpenters from eleven different cities. Together, these carpenters formed a national union, complete with its own constitution. Two thousand members could be accounted for right from the start. Today, the union is a strong and powerful economic and political force for setting wages and benefits and for setting standards of conditions and quality for all carpentry projects in the United States.

According to the UBC's Web site, "The UBC represents and offers training to North America's carpenters, cabinetmakers, millwrights, piledrivers, lathers, framers, floor layers, roofers, drywallers, and workers in forest-products and related industries."

CHAPTER 2

ELECTRICIAN

A n electrician installs, operates, or repairs electrical equipment. Without electricity, many of the systems we take for granted would not exist: lights, computers, refrigerators, and televisions. All are powered by electricity. But just how do you think the electricity gets there? Well, that is the job of the highly skilled electrician.

A Professional Electrician's Viewpoint

Will Munroe is a journeyman inside wireman (a type of electrician) in Detroit, Michigan. He recounts some of his job experiences:

> I've had a few experiences where I had to correct somebody's handiwork. The most common problem that people have is with two switches that control the same light fixture. Generally, that's no big deal. I have had to correct some more serious problems also. Some things will not work correctly if wired wrong. This can be a hazard depending on what it is. The most serious

issue is grounding. If an electrical device such as an outlet or an appliance is not grounded properly, it can result in injury or death. As little as 50 milliamps of current can kill a person, depending on the duration of the shock and the path it takes through the body. Fifty milliamps is the amount of power to light up a six-watt lightbulb, such as a small Christmas tree light. I've also seen people use the wrong size wire for what was needed. If the wire is not big enough, it will get hot. This will lead to a fire. When in doubt, call an electrician!

INSIDE, OUTSIDE, UPSIDE DOWN?

There are four sub-jobs, so to speak, that fall under the umbrella term "electrician." Each is a specialty, a particular type of electrician, trained to do a unique type of electrical work.

According to the U.S. Department of Labor, the inside wireman is an electrical worker who installs the power, the lighting, various controls, and other electrical equipment in commercial and industrial buildings. The outside lineman is an electrical worker who installs distribution and transmission lines that move power from the power plant to homes, businesses, and factories. A residential wireman is an electrical worker who specializes in the installation of all the electrical systems in homes. Finally, the voice-data-video installer technician, or more simply, the installer technician, is an electrical worker who installs circuits and equipment for telephones, computer networks, video distribution systems, security, and access control systems and other low-voltage systems.

THE INSIDE WIREMAN

According to the National Joint Apprenticeship and Training Committee of National Electrical Contractors Association (NJATC) and the International Brotherhood

The Duties of an Inside Wireman

99% Installing new wiring and repairing old wiring

98% Installing receptacles, lighting systems, and fixtures

97% Planning and installing raceway systems

94% Troubleshooting and repairing electrical systems

92% Planning and initiating projects

92% Supervising journeymen and apprentices

88% Establishing temporary power during construction

88% Establishing power distribution within projects

87% Establishing grounding systems

86% Installing service to buildings and other structures

86% Providing power and controls to motors, HVAC, and other equipment

82% Installing fire alarm systems

71% Installing and repairing traffic signals, outdoor lighting, and outdoor power feeders

67% Establishing OSHA and customer safety requirements

67% Installing instrumentation and process control systems, including energy management systems

64% Erecting and assembling power generation equipment

57% Installing security systems

56% Installing, maintaining, and repairing lightning protection systems

36% Installing and repairing telephone and data systems

of Electrical Workers (IBEW), the breakdown of duties performed by the inside wireman is as explained in the chart above (the number next to each duty shows the percentage of journeymen who perform that task).

While the outside lineman works on the distribution network bringing power from sources of generation to the customers, the inside wireman is charged with the task of distributing and connecting his or her customer's electrical equipment to the power source that was installed by the outside lineman. The inside wireman is responsible for the installation and the maintenance of the different types of electrical systems that are commonly found in both commercial and industrial facilities. Examples of these electrical systems are motors, heating equipment, lighting, and systems controlling the operation of all the facility's energy usage.

The inside wireman also installs conduit systems. These systems contain the wire from the panel boards (or motor control centers) to each piece of equipment within the facility that uses electricity. These conduits are the containers for power cables and control cables. Because many of the conduit systems are exposed, they require precise installation according to exact standards. They must also be installed neatly and look professional when complete.

Aside from this, the actual tasks performed by the inside wireman vary somewhat. For example, he or she

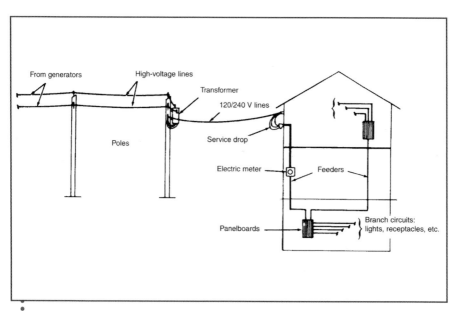

This diagram depicts a home's basic electric systems and shows the entrance of electrical service into a home, the feeders and lines to subpanels, and branch circuits. The outside lineman generally deals with the transmission lines that carry power from a generating plant to a local service point. The residential wireman usually installs and maintains the electrical systems within a home.

might install a conduit in a ditch outside of a building. Later in the week, he or she might install security or fire alarm systems for an office building. It would not be unusual for the inside wireman to find him- or herself installing the electrical systems for various industrial facilities, including automobile, chemical, and power plants, and chip manufacturing facilities.

Each one of the different types of electrical system installations performed by the inside wireman carries its own precise set of electrical needs with accompanying systems, which support those needs.

There are specific tasks that fall under the job description of the inside wireman. While doing an apprenticeship, the soon-to-be inside wireman receives the training and knowledge necessary to do each task professionally and skillfully.

The inside wireman is skilled at using a large number of different tools. While some tools are used more frequently than others, a wide variety of hand tools and power tools, meters, and heavy equipment are used by the skilled electrician. The Web site of the National Joint Apprenticeship and Training Committee lists the following tools as those used by electricians.

Hand Tools

- Adapter cables
- Allen wrench
- Architect scale
- Block and tackle (the ropes or chains used for hoisting tackle)
- Caliper (an instrument for measuring thicknesses and internal or external diameters inaccessible to a scale, consisting usually of a pair of adjustable pivoted legs)
- Clamps
- Crimping tools

- File
- Fuse pullers
- Hacksaw
- Hammer
- Hand bender
- Hand drill
- Hand reamer (any of various rotary tools, with heads that have teeth or grooves)
- Handsaw
- Hoist (an apparatus for hoisting, as a block and tackle, a derrick, or a crane)
- Keyhole saw
- Knife
- Ladder
- Level
- Measuring tape
- Needle nose pliers
- Pipe wrench
- Pliers
- Plumb bob
- Punch
- Ruler
- Screwdriver
- Shovel
- Slip joint pliers (a gripping hand tool with a joint adjustable to two positions in order to increase the opening of the jaws).
- Socket set
- Tamp tool (a tool used to force something in or down by repeated, rather light strokes)
- Torque wrench
- Transit (an instrument used for measuring horizontal and sometimes vertical angles)
- Vise
- Wire cutters
- Wire stripper

- Wood chisel
- Wrench

POWER-ASSISTED TOOLS

- Air hammer
- Coring machine to drill through concrete
- Drill press
- Electric roto hammer drill
- Electric saber saw
- Electric screw gun
- Fiber-optic fusion splicer
- Gas-operated auger
- Hand drill
- Hydraulic bender
- Power cutting and threading machine
- Roto stripper
- Soldering iron
- Water pump
- Wire tugger

METERS

- Ammeter (an instrument for measuring current in amperes)
- Dynamometer (a device for measuring mechanical force or power)
- Megger (a portable instrument used to measure insulation resistance)
- Optical power meter
- Optical time-domain reflectometer (a special piece of fiber-optic equipment that can trace and record weaknesses and breaks in a fiber-optic cable)
- Oscilloscope (a device that uses a cathode-ray tube or similar instrument to depict on a screen periodic changes in an electric quantity, as voltage or current)

- Voltmeter (a calibrated instrument for measuring the potential difference between two points)
- Wattmeter (a calibrated instrument for measuring electric power in watts)

Heavy Equipment

- Auger
- Back hoe
- Bucket truck
- Caterpillar (a tractor), earth-moving equipment, etc., propelled by Caterpillar treads
- Crane
- Derrick (a hoisting apparatus similar to a crane)
- Dozer
- Electric lift
- Power borer
- Trencher

Two Electricians Offer Their Insights About Their Careers

Scott McDanel, Journeyman Inside Wireman

Scott McDanel, thirty-seven, of Colona, Illinois, works as an electrician. Specifically, he is a journeyman inside wireman. He does installation and maintenance of electrical equipment.

I am an inside wireman. The basic difference between an inside wireman and an outside wireman is that an outside wireman works with power lines. Inside wiremen still work outside doing traffic signals and parking-lot lights and such, but usually we only have to deal with voltages of 480 volts that are three-phase and below. We do mess with higher voltages at times but it is rare.

My primary responsibility is to wire power and lighting diagrams from scratch. I am also responsible for trouble shooting the various systems.

I was an apprentice for five years before I became a journeyman wireman. That was mandatory. I completed the apprenticeship . . . and learned the greatest deal of the technical aspects from hands-on training.

Aside from classroom instruction, one must complete 8,000 on-the-job training hours where most aspects of the job will be covered. Before that, I was already a college graduate with a military background. I have a bachelor's degree in electronics and energy and power. I had to take a pre-entrance exam to get into school to become an electrician. Now I carry a journeyman electrician card that states I have completed the apprenticeship. And I belong to IBEW Local 145. The guidelines of IBEW Local 145 state that a member must be in good standing and carry a drug free certification card. [The IBEW, or International Brotherhood of Electrical Workers, is a union. Local IBEW unions are numbered.]

When asked about personal qualifications for his job, McDanel says, "It helps to be physically fit." About the salary range for his position, McDanel explained:

As you begin as a first-year apprentice you are probably at about $12 an hour with percentage increments as you progress through the apprenticeship. Once journeyman status is met, depending on the overtime that may be available for you to work, one can make between $50,000 and $80,000 a year.

The work environments I have encountered are a broad range of everything from the cleanest office in the world to a mud hole of a new foundation.

McDanel is optimistic about the future of the trade. "There is always a need for lighting and power, thus the

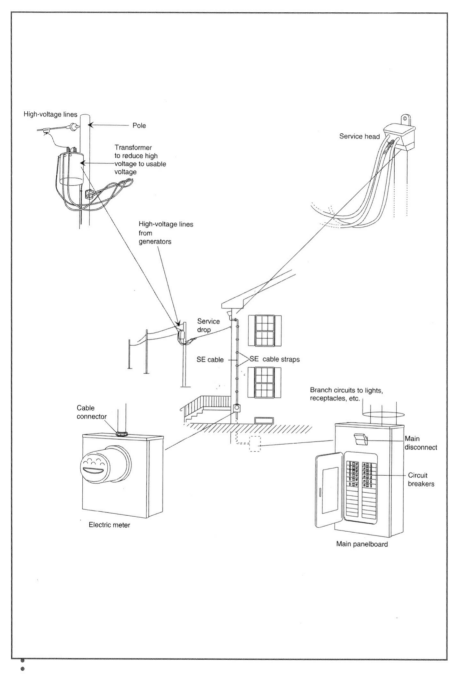

This figure from an electricians' exam preparation guide illustrates the basic components of an electric service, including the service drop, service conductors, and main panel boards.

4-1 The overhead conductors, through which electrical service is supplied, between the last power company pole and the building or other support used for the purpose are called:

A) Service entrance

B) Service-entrance conductors

C) Service drop

D) Service-entrance equipment

Answer: C

NEC Article 100 — Definitions. See Figure 4-1.

4-2 The conductors and equipment for delivering electric energy from the power company to the wiring system of the premises served is called a:

A) Service

B) Service-entrance conductors

C) Service drop

D) Service-entrance equipment

Answer: A

NEC Article 100 — Definitions. See Figure 4-1.

4-3 The conductors between the point of termination of the overhead service drop or underground service lateral and the main disconnecting device in a building are known as:

A) Service

B) Service conductors

C) Service drop

D) Service-entrance equipment

Answer: B

NEC Article 100 — Definitions. See Figure 4-1.

4-4 The necessary equipment connected to the load end of the service conductors to a building or other structure and intended to constitute the main control and cutoff of the supply is known as:

A) Service entrance

B) Service-entrance conductors

C) Service drop

D) Service equipment

Answer: D

NEC Article 100 — Definitions. See Figure 4-1.

The test questions listed above are samples from an electricians' exam preparation guide. The four questions and answers relate to the figure reproduced on the opposite page.

outlook is good." He recommends visiting the IBEW Local 145 Web site to anyone interested in working as an electrician: http://www.ibewlocal145.com.

WILL MUNROE, JOURNEYMAN INSIDE WIREMAN

Will Munroe, thirty-two, of Detroit, describes his duties as an electrician, specifically a journeyman inside wireman.

> *My responsibilities vary. I work on computer cabling and fiber optics to traffic signals to new residential, commercial and industrial construction, service work, and numerous other things. My other responsibilities are that I have to perform the work, interact with the customers and the electrical inspector, I have to order materials, do various types of paperwork, and I have to coordinate my work with other trades.*

About the future in this industry, Will says:

> *To be honest, I think it is somewhat questionable with the shape of the economy as it is. Many companies are relocating and not building or expanding. The residential market is still strong, however.*

About his prior training, Will explains:

> *Before I decided to become an electrician, I was a recent college graduate with a four-year degree in an unrelated field. When I decided to become an electrician, I found out that I had to complete an apprenticeship program. I needed a high school diploma with one year of college algebra to get into my apprenticeship program. I already had those, so I was able to get started right away. There is a basic aptitude test to get into the apprenticeship program. You must also interview. It is very competitive. Hundreds of*

people apply in the area in which I live, and maybe eight or ten people may get into the program each year. I had to complete a five-year apprenticeship program that included over 1,000 hours of classroom instruction and over 10,000 hours of on-the-job training. I learned a lot during my apprenticeship. I learned the skills I needed for the job. I learned how to work with others. I also learned a lot from other people. And I learned how to teach other people.

Now that he is an electrician, Will explains:

Some areas have local license requirements, and some states have license requirements. It varies. I have a certificate from the National Joint Apprenticeship and Training Committee, which is regulated by the federal government. I am a member of the International Brotherhood of Electrical Workers Union.

The work environment can be very physically demanding at times. You work with your hands a lot, so you must have good eye-hand coordination. Mechanical aptitude is needed, too.

THE OUTSIDE LINEMAN

The outside lineman is a bit of a construction worker in the field of electricity. He or she constructs the transmission lines that carry power from remote generating plants all the way to local service areas.

While working under close supervision of a journeyman lineman, the apprentice outside lineman learns how to work safely in his or her trade. The most important thing to know as an electrician is how to avoid being electrocuted while on the job.

Outside linemen must be strong and agile, as they are often required to climb to reach the tops of wooden poles. On some occasions, the outside lineman has the luxury of working from a bucket truck. But on those occasions when a bucket truck is not available or practical, climbing is required. A good outside lineman is also not averse to working in inclement weather conditions. It will not be unusual to find oneself working through a storm to keep the power up and running. This is especially important for hospitals, but homes, schools, and factories certainly appreciate the work of outside linemen as well.

INSTALLER TECHNICIAN

The installer technician works closely with the inside wireman. He or she is busy installing the network of low-voltage cabling. This is the type of cable used commonly for things that require low-voltage signaling, such as video, voice, and data. Most of the time, the installer technician is working inside buildings, which offers protection from the weather. However, because the installer technician is often working before the heat and air-conditioning systems and the lighting system are installed, working conditions are still often less than favorable. Not all jobs are on new, incomplete buildings, luckily for the installer. Just as often, he or she might find him- or herself at work inside an office building. However, the installer may also find him- or herself at work outside, fair game for any weather.

The installer technician works to route data and voice cable. These must run from a spot outside the building to the telephone and equipment rooms inside and then from there to the separate workstations throughout the building. According to the NJATC:

The installer technician installs voice and data outlets at workstations. In addition, they install punch down blocks [devices that connect one group of wires to another group of wires through a system of metal pegs that the wires are attached to] and cross connects in telephone rooms. These may be wall mounted or rack mounted, and must be grouped and identified according to specific installation standards. Whether the work is in new construction or in existing office or manufacturing space, the IBEW-NECA craftsman takes pride in the work he or she has and can perform. The NJATC trains to TIA/EIA (Telecommunications Industries Association [TIA] and Electronic Industries Alliance [EIA]) and other industry standards. The NJATC also partners with the major manufacturers in the video, voice, and data industry to assure training in the latest technologies, including training for manufacturers warranted installs.

The installer technician performs many different types of electrical installations. While every installer is not a specialist in all these types of systems, most installers are trained to work on several different types of installations. The installer technician will be expected to complete tasks that could include installing communications and sound distribution systems and pathways and spaces for low-voltage wiring, installing underground voice or data circuit feeders to entrance facilities, and installing, terminating, and testing copper and fiber-optic wires and cables. Other jobs involve installing, testing, and certifying local area network (LAN) cabling systems and laying out, installing, and verifying operation of security and access control systems.

Additional installation-related tasks include planning and initiating projects, assembling telecommunications racks for field installation, connecting to the grounding electrode system, and providing testing, analysis, and repair of video, voice, and data systems, including electronic devices such as gateways, routers, hubs, network interface cards, and telephone switches. Installers might also work on other subsystems, such as communications, entertainment, environmental, life safety, energy management, and custom lighting.

RESIDENTIAL WIREMAN

The final example of a type of electrician is the residential wireman. A residential wireman's job is similar to the work of an inside wireman. Like the inside wireman, the residential wireman will install systems that also distribute electricity from one source to all pieces of machinery within a building that need power from this source. However, while the inside wireman does work on large buildings, the residential wireman, as the job title implies, works on homes.

In recent years, the work of the residential wireman has expanded to meet the needs of the ever-growing world of technology. Residential wiremen are now capable of installing systems for computers, security, and fire alarms, in addition to the usual light and energy systems used in homes.

Like the inside wireman, the residential wireman may know how to do any of the tasks listed below but will probably specialize in certain ones.

- Install and verify operation of security, fire alarm, and access control systems
- Install and work on other subsystems such as heating/air-conditioning, solar voltaic generation, and energy management systems
- Install local area network systems
- Install pathways and circuit conductors for power distribution
- Install pathways and spaces for installation of low-voltage wiring
- Install sound and cable TV distribution systems
- Install underground power circuit and telephone feeders to entrance facilities
- Provide or connect to the grounding electrode system
- Test, certify, and troubleshoot all system wiring installations

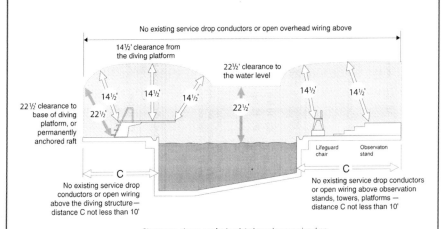

No existing service drop conductors or open overhead wiring above

14½' clearance from the diving platform

22½' clearance to the water level

14½'   14½'   14½'   14½'   14½'

22½' clearance to base of diving platform, or permanently anchored raft

22½'   22½'   22½'

Lifeguard chair   Observaton stand

C

No existing service drop conductors or open wiring above the diving structure— distance C not less than 10'

C

No existing service drop conductors or open wiring above observation stands, towers, platforms — distance C not less than 10'

Clearances shown are for insulated supply or service drop cables, 0-750 volts to ground, supported on and cabled together with an effectively grounded bare messenger or effectively grounded neutral conductor

---

11-9 Lighting fixtures above a pool without GFCI protection must be installed at a minimum height of:

A) 5 feet

B) 2 feet

C) 10 feet

D) 12 feet

Answer: D

11-10 In general, overhead conductors must not pass directly over a pool or horizontally within how many feet of the inside walls of the pool?

A) 5 feet

B) 18 feet

C) 10 feet

D) 3 feet

Answer: C

This diagram showing the clearances for overhead conductors above swimming pools, 750 volts or less, and the related test questions listed below the diagram are examples from an electricians' exam preparation guide. The National Electrical Code (NEC) provides rules for safely installing electrical wiring in or near swimming pools. The abbreviation GFCI in question 11-9 refers to ground fault circuit interrupt, a safety device that works like a circuit breaker.

A License to Electrify

Most electricians are required to carry a license to practice electrical work. Depending on the specific type of work the electrician does, he or she may have one or more of the following classes of license:

- Apprentice
- Contractor
- Journeyman
- Lineman
- Master
- Wireman

Each of these licenses can be further specialized for commercial work, residential work, maintenance, and work on a manufacturing plant.

As explained by electrician Will Munroe:

These are classifications, but not necessarily of licenses themselves. An apprentice doesn't have a license. They have to work and go to school for up to five years. After the apprenticeship, you are usually called a journeyman. A contractor is the person who owns the business. Some states or cities require a contractor to have a license, and that license covers anybody who works for his company. Some states and/or cities require each individual to have his or her own license. A journeyman and a wireman are about the same. A lineman is an electrician who works outside, such as on power poles, high voltage (up to 300,000 volts), and on transformers. Master electrician is another term that is interchangeable with journeyman. Different places use these terms to classify people.

The actual requirements to obtain an electrician's license are somewhat different (although not drastically different) depending on the area in which you work.

However, in general, electricians are required to pass an exam that tests their knowledge of electrical theory, building codes, local electrical codes, and the National Electrical Code. The National Electrical Code, or NEC, [is] a book that defines terms and words used by people who work in the electrical industry and lists approved materials and methods to be used in the trade. This book, which is updated every three years, deals with standards for things such as grounding, wire gauge, and minimum branch circuit protection, for example. It is used to plan the work to be done, and it tells how things are to be done and the proper way things are to be used. The NEC is generally accepted by everybody that enforces the code. Most cities use this book as their guide for the electrical inspectors to follow. Some places supplement the code with additional requirements or tougher standards. One of the most important functions of the NEC is to protect people.

The type of license an electrician carries depends on his or her education in the field as well as his or her experience in the field. The type of license is based on required education and work experience. Different states have different guidelines. Massachusetts, for example, has specific guidelines under which those who have gained experience doing electrical work while in the armed forces are considered license-worthy. You will have to contact your own state to find out exactly what is required of electricians to obtain a license to work, as each state may have somewhat different licensing requirements.

TRAINING THE ELECTRICIAN

Many electricians learn their trade by watching someone in their family work. Then they try out a few things on their own. How does this work? How does the electricity get from here to there? How can I make this machine work? A keen mind and a healthy curiosity drive the would-be electrician to seek a career in electricity. The majority of electricians are graduates of four-year or five-year apprentice programs.

During the apprenticeship, the electrician-in-training gains experience and a full knowledge of every aspect and nuance of the electrical industry. The apprenticeship also greatly increases his or her odds of landing a job as an electrician. When it comes to apprenticeships, electricians have the market cornered. More electricians learn their trade through apprenticeships than do the workers in other construction trades. That said, it must also be noted that many electricians learn the skills of their trade while on the job.

You can visit the NJATC Web site (http://www.njatc.org) to look at the listing of courses that you can take online. Details regarding the courses and enrollment can be found at the Web site. Whether you pick up the skills of electrical work by watching relatives or friends work, on the job, or through an apprentice program, if you want to get a job, you will want to have some sort of training. Several courses, which are typically offered in most high schools, are recommended. These include electricity, electronics, mathematics, mechanical drawing, and science.

Two types of apprenticeship programs offer training to would-be electricians. One of these is the Union-Employer Program.

According to the U.S. Department of Labor Veterans' Employment and Training Service:

Large apprenticeship programs are usually sponsored by joint training committees made up of local unions of the International Brotherhood of Electrical Workers (IBEW) and local chapters of the National Electrical Contractors Association (NECA). Union membership is required. The National Joint Apprentice and Training

Committee (NJATC) is a joint program of the IBEW and the NECA and has hundreds of local programs offering apprenticeship and training in the following areas: Residential Wireman, Journeyman Lineman, Journeyman Tree Trimmer, Journeyman Inside Wireman, Advanced Journeyman Training, and Telecommunication Installer-Technician.

The other type of apprenticeship program that offers training to would-be electricians is the Non-Union Program. Committees of individual electrical contracting companies may offer electrician training. Local chapters of the Associated Builders and Contractors and the Independent Electrical Contractors also offer electrician training programs. Because you will learn so many aspects of electrical work while you are in your apprenticeship, you will be qualified and have the appropriate knowledge to work on both maintenance and construction projects.

Most of the larger apprenticeship programs provide a minimum of 144 hours of classroom instruction per year, plus an additional 8,000 hours of on-the-job training, which are spread out over the entire course of the apprenticeship. Depending on where you live, you may find slight variances in the basic requirements for apprenticeship programs. However, in order to qualify for most apprenticeships, applicants must meet at least two common requirements. They must be at least eighteen years old, and they must have either a high school diploma or a GED. The GED, or general equivalency diploma, is a test a person may take to receive an equivalent of a high school diploma if he or she has failed to complete coursework and graduate from high school.

The U.S. Bureau of Apprenticeship and Training (BAT), an agency of the U.S. Department of Labor, registers apprenticeship programs and apprentices in twenty-three states, and assists and oversees State Apprenticeship

Councils (SACs) that perform these functions in the remaining twenty-seven states and the District of Columbia. Registering an apprenticeship program means that the employer, employer association, or joint employer/union partnership is accepted and recorded by the BAT or an SAC. To qualify for registration, an apprenticeship program needs to meet either the standards and requirements of certain federal regulations in the state where the BAT is the registration agency, or the standards and requirements instituted by that state if an SAC is the registration agency. The labor standards generally include safeguarding the welfare of apprentices and setting the policies and procedures involving the apprenticeship programs. For the most part, each local electrician apprenticeship program has to meet the requirements of the BAT registered model. Nevertheless, there are some variations that are allowed to accommodate specific programs to meet individual needs. Some local electrical programs, for example, require a fifth year, or a total of 10,000 hours of on-the-job training, to complete the apprenticeship. People who finish BAT or SAC registered programs frequently have received training in both electrical installation and electrical maintenance applications.

While in the classroom, an apprentice will most likely learn a number of important skills. Among these are blueprint reading, electrical code requirements, electrical theory, electronics, first-aid practices, mathematics, and safety practices. In addition, he or she will receive specialized training in welding, fire alarm systems, and communications. Then, when the apprentice does his or her on-the-job training under the direct supervision of experienced electricians, he or she will gain experience and skill in:

- Drilling holes, setting anchors, and conduit
- Measuring, fabricating, and installing conduit, wiring, outlets, and switches

- Setting up and drawing diagrams for entire electrical systems

As previously mentioned, the electrician may also seek informal training. He or she may choose to gain the necessary skills by working for experienced electricians, by taking courses at a local trade school, or by enrolling in a correspondence program.

Another great place to pick up training is in the armed forces. Technical schools offer excellent training as well.

If you are considering a career as a maintenance electrician, it will be useful for you to gain experience with electronics due to the increasingly frequent use of complex electronic controls on manufacturing equipment.

SAMPLE A TEST

Before you sit for your big electrician exam, you may want to be sure that you will pass. Of course, you should know everything you need to know from your time as an apprentice. But sometimes it helps to have a little bit of an extra edge. There are courses designed especially for helping you prepare for your exam. These preparation courses can even be found online for your convenience. One such online course can be found on Electrician.com. For a nominal fee, you can take its Online Journeyman Electrician License Test Course.

The course is divided into two parts, which are based on the 2005 National Electrical Code. The course is a resource of more than 2,000 electrical test questions, plus articles and electrical books. The coursework was prepared by a former state electrical inspector. You can take the 2004 practice test, which is available on the Web site. Included with the test is a section of supplemental materials, such as a test-taking guide, basic electrical theory for electricians, and "material that you should know before taking an Electrician's Test."

JOIN A PROFESSIONAL ORGANIZATION

When you have become an electrician, you will want to look into all of the organizations that refer to your new field of work. Electrician.com provides links to thirteen different electrician-related organizations. For example, there is a link that takes you to the Occupational Safety and Health Administration (OSHA) Web site. This site has articles regarding safety issues in the field of electrical work, as supplied by this agency of the United States Department of Labor.

Another link will direct you to the Institute of Electrical and Electronics Engineers, Inc. (IEEE). This technical professional association has more than 360,000 members who live in 175 countries. According to the IEEE's Web site,

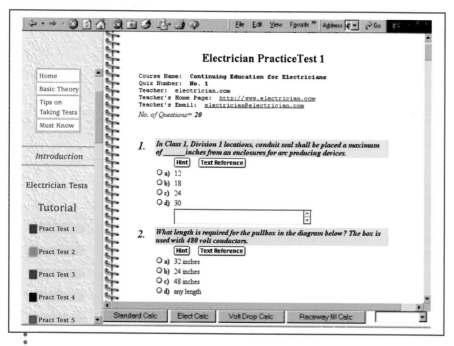

A practice electricians' test to help a journeyman to prepare for a licensing examination is available on Electrician.com.

"Through its members, the IEEE is a leading authority in technical areas ranging from computer engineering, bio-medical technology, and telecommunications, to electric power, aerospace and consumer electronics, among others." Members of the IEEE are privileged to the following benefits:

- Membership in one or more of thirty-seven IEEE societies and four technical councils spanning the range of electrotechnologies and information technologies
- More than 300 local organizations worldwide for member networking and information sharing
- Educational opportunities to ensure engineers' technical vitality
- Public advocacy for U.S. member interests and for women in engineering and ethics
- More than 1,150 student branches at universities worldwide
- Special cost-saving and value-added benefits for members only
- Prestigious awards and recognition of technical and professional achievements
- Opportunities for volunteering, leadership, and participation in a variety of IEEE activities
- Electronic commerce with the IEEE through a variety of Web-based services

According to the IEEE's Web site, the organization was founded in 1884 by:

[E]lectrical engineering innovators who understood the value of shared information. The IEEE vision is to advance global prosperity by fostering technological innovation, enabling members' careers, and promoting community worldwide. Members of the IEEE lead the world to new technical developments, formulate internationally recognized standards, and shape the global community.

An Electrifying History

Although your interest in electricity has already brought you to this chapter in this book, taking a look back at the history of electricity is going to make you even more interested!

Electricity Online is a Web site worth visiting for students who wish to learn more about theory and practical applications of electricity. This Web site (http://library.thinkquest.org/28032) is full of all sorts of things electrical, from history to learning sessions that conclude in fun, game-style checking of your knowledge. This is a great site to visit even if you are still only thinking about becoming an electrician.

CHAPTER 3

PLUMBER

A plumber installs or repairs plumbing. "Plumb" is from the Latin word for "lead," the material from which buildings' pipes were once made.

The job descriptions of the plumber and his or her counterpart, the pipe fitter, are roughly the same. Thus, if you are considering work as a pipe fitter, the following information will benefit you as well.

SO YOU THINK YOU WANT TO BE A PLUMBER

Everyone uses plumbing on a regular basis, day in and day out. But have you ever thought about how the plumbing systems in your bathroom and kitchen work? Yes, there is a system of pipes that brings clean water in and takes dirty water out. That's the basic idea. Most people wonder no further about their plumbing, unless of course the kitchen sink is clogged with food or the toilet won't flush! Then even the most squeamish wishes he or she were a plumber!

If you have ever taken apart a sink's pipes to remove a clog and thought the process challenging, if you have ever helped install a bathtub and found the project rewarding, or if you have ever flushed the toilet and wondered just where all that, er, stuff goes, perhaps a career in the plumbing industry is for you!

PLUMBING IN NINETEENTH-CENTURY AMERICA

If you think back to the 1800s, you will get a mental picture of log cabins behind which were usually two very important things: a stream with fresh running water or a water pump, and the all-important outhouse. You may also have an image of family members lined up to take their weekly bath in the family's tin washtub. One family member is in the bucket while another pours water, heated over a fire, over the head of the bather. Indoor plumbing was on the horizon, but throughout the majority of the nineteenth century, Americans typically had only primitive plumbing. Students who are interested in learning more about the history of plumbing in America can visit the PlumbingSupply.com Web site (http://www.plumbingsupply.com/pmamerica.html).

THE PLUMBER

Plumbers work with a range of materials and fixtures that are used to plan, repair, install, remove, extend, alter, and/or maintain plumbing systems. Included under the blanket term "plumbing systems" are all fixtures that supply water, drainage, and waste removal, such as storm drainage, venting systems, sanitary drainage systems, public and private water systems, and the gas piping that is part of any building. In addition, venting or hot liquid heating is also part of plumbing systems.

A PLUMBER'S WORK

Depending on several aspects of the field, a plumber may or may not decide to specialize in his or her work. If a plumber has a specific interest or a particular skill level, that person may choose to specialize in that area. He or she may want to work solely as an installer of plumbing for new houses, for example. Or he or she may be great at maintenance, repair, and renovation of plumbing that another plumber has already installed. In general, plumbers work not only with pipes and water but with heating and drainage systems as well. Their work may include any of the following tasks: connecting plumbing fixtures, radiators, and water heaters; installing air-conditioning units, heating units, bathtubs, dishwashers, garbage disposals, hot water tanks, and sinks; repairing bathtubs, dishwashers, garbage disposals, hot water tanks, and sinks; replacing burst water pipes; and working on septic tanks and sewers.

Plumbers who work in large cities have a better chance of being able to specialize their work. Plumbers working in small towns may find it necessary to be good at everything, from private home plumbing to water distribution system plumbing.

In addition to an interest in water and pipes and how things in a plumbing system work, there are several other job requirements, besides owning a heavy-duty plunger, that must be met before you land your job in plumbing. If you wish to find work as a plumber, you should:

- Have a high school diploma or a GED
- Be at least eighteen years old
- Be physically fit and capable to do the work
- Have a valid driver's license
- Have proof that you are legally allowed to work in the United States
- Be able to read, write, and speak English

The last qualification is important so that you will be able to understand the instructions in school and for each project you do, as well as understand safety precautions to take during your work to ensure not only your own well-being but that of your coworkers.

In addition to the above requirements, training in plumbing while in the armed forces is recognized and may even count as previous credit when joining an apprenticeship program once discharged, according to the

---

8-7 The interceptor shown in Figure 8-1 is required by Code to prevent _____ from entering into the building drainage system.

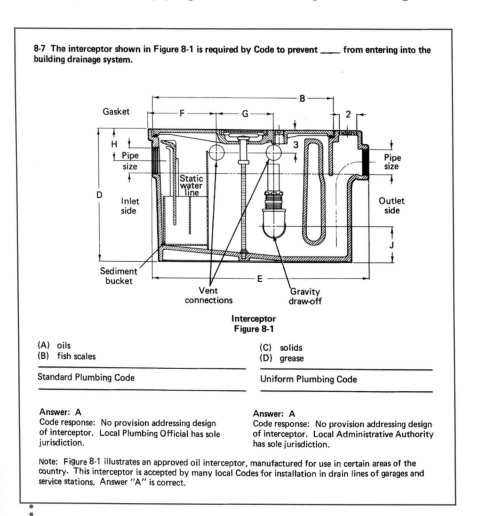

Interceptor
Figure 8-1

(A) oils
(B) fish scales

(C) solids
(D) grease

Standard Plumbing Code

Uniform Plumbing Code

Answer: A
Code response: No provision addressing design of interceptor. Local Plumbing Official has sole jurisdiction.

Answer: A
Code response: No provision addressing design of interceptor. Local Administrative Authority has sole jurisdiction.

Note: Figure 8-1 illustrates an approved oil interceptor, manufactured for use in certain areas of the country. This interceptor is accepted by many local Codes for installation in drain lines of garages and service stations. Answer "A" is correct.

This drawing from a plumbers' exam preparation guide shows an approved oil interceptor used in many types of garage and service station plumbing drainage systems. An interceptor is a device for separating oil from the drainage system so that the oil does not enter the sewage system.

U.S. Department of Labor Veterans' Employment and Training Service.

A plumber must be strong enough to lift and fit heavy pipes, stand on his or her feet to work for long hours at a stretch, and often work in cramped positions. He or she must like to work with tools and equipment. A plumber should enjoy working on tasks that require a great deal of accuracy and precision. He or she needs to be good at solving problems. He or she should be able to work well alone and with a group. He or she should be able to follow directions well and respect the rules of plumbing.

The U.S. Department of Labor's Bureau of Apprenticeship and Training registers apprenticeship training programs in twenty-three states. It also lists training programs with

---

20-11 You are cutting four pieces of pipe end-to-end, with the following dimensions: 3′2-1/4″, 4′7-3/8″, 5′4-5/8″, 6′6-7/8″. To make these cuts, you would need _____ of pipe. Select the closest answer.

(A) 19′6″

(B) 19′10-1/8″

(C) 19′-9″

(D) 20′2-3/16″

Answer: C

Solution: Change all feet into inches. Also change inches into decimals where appropriate.

Fraction	=	Decimal
1/4	=	.250
3/8	=	.375
5/8	=	.625
7/8	=	.875

$$3′2\text{-}1/4″ = (3 \times 12″ = 36″ + 2″ + .25″) = 38.250″$$
$$4′7\text{-}3/8″ = (4 \times 12″ = 48″ + 7″ + .375″) = 55.375″$$
$$5′4\text{-}5/8″ = (5 \times 12″ = 60″ + 4″ + .625″) = 64.625″$$
$$6′6\text{-}7/8″ = (6 \times 12″ = 72″ + 6″ + .875″) = 78.875″$$

Total inches   237.125″

$$\frac{237.125″}{12″/ft.} = 19.76′, \text{ or approximately } 19\tfrac{3}{4}′ \text{ which is } 19′9″$$

Plumbers should have excellent skills in mathematics. This sample test question for an apprentice, journeyman, or master plumber requires a test taker to change feet into inches and inches into decimals before answering the question.

state apprenticeship councils in about twenty-seven states and the District of Columbia, and supervises these councils.

Once the plumber-in-training completes his or her registered apprenticeship program, he or she will receive certification, which proves that he or she has completed the program. Accepted throughout the plumbing industry, this certificate is good across the country because each registered apprenticeship program is based on a set of formal standards. Once a plumber graduates from his or her registered apprenticeship program, he or she is considered qualified to take journey-level positions, which are subject to local examination and licensing requirements.

WORKING CONDITIONS

Depending on the actual job, the conditions in which a plumber works can vary. Working indoors is certainly more favorable to most plumbers. However, plumbers often find themselves working outdoors as well. If working in construction (as opposed to maintenance), plumbers can expect to find more work during the summer months while the weather is warm. The hours will be long. Plumbers must be strong enough to lift heavy pipes and other supplies and equipment. Plumbers are at some risk for accidents and injuries on the job because they work with power tools, pipe-joining equipment, and rough metals.

WHAT'S THE PAY?

The average plumber makes around $20 per hour. Apprentices earn a minimum of about $12 per hour. According to author Paul Phifer in his book *Great Careers in 2 Years* (2003), the average plumber's salary ranges from

National Estimates for Plumbers, Pipefitters, and Steamfitters as Reported in May 2003 by the U.S. Department of Labor, Bureau of Labor Statistics

Employment estimate and mean wage estimates for this occupation:

Employment (1)	Employment RSE (3)	Mean hourly wage	Mean annual wage (2)	Wage RSE (3)
433,600	1.4 %	$20.89	$43,450	0.7 %

Percentile wage estimates for this occupation:

Percentile	10%	25%	50% (Median)	75%	90%
Hourly Wage	$11.33	$14.83	$19.69	$26.44	$33.17
Annual Wage (2)	$23,570	$30,840	$40,950	$55,000	$68,990

1. Estimates for detailed occupations do not sum to the totals because the totals include occupations not shown separately. Estimates do not include self-employed workers.
2. Annual wages have been calculated by multiplying the hourly mean wage by a year-round, full-time hours figure of 2,080 hours.
3. The relative standard error (RSE) is a measure of the reliability of a survey statistic. The smaller the relative standard error, the more precise the estimate.

$22,000 to $63,000 and up. According to Salary.com, the range in salary that a plumber can expect to earn is based on the type and duration of the job he or she does. An average base salary is just over $44,000 with about half of all plumbers earning from $39,538 to $48,383 per year.

GET TO WORK

While some plumbers may be self-employed, many plumbers work for construction contractors or for plumbing repair shops and other large plumbing businesses. After having worked a while in the plumbing industry, a plumber may decide to start his or her own business. Or, if he or she is happy with his or her current employer and wishes to remain with the company, he or she may have the opportunity to become the supervisor, who in plumbing is called the foreman or the estimator. A plumber who wishes to use his or her skills to become a safety codes officer, also known as an inspector, can get some additional training. Information about such training can be obtained from the Safety Codes Council, National Skills Standards Board Institute, 1441 L Street NW, Suite 9000, Washington, D.C., 20005-3512.

TRAINING TO BECOME A PLUMBER: THE APPRENTICESHIP

To become a plumber, one must take a Trade Entrance Exam and in some states, such as Oregon, score at least 75 percent. Once this has been accomplished, the potential plumber must find a professional plumber who is willing and able to teach him or her the tricks of the trade. In other words, he or she must be willing to hire the soon-to-be-plumber and teach him or her all he or she needs to know about the field of plumbing. Thus the soon-to-be-plumber becomes the plumber's apprentice. He or she will work in this position for three or four years (the period varies from state to state), during which time he or she will have four employment terms of at least 1,800 hours each. He or she is also required to take four training classes, each eight weeks long. He or she may also choose to attend an additional classroom training

16-23 When installing a gas range, the Code mandates that an accessible gas shut-off valve be installed upstream from the union or range connector. Distance "X" in Figure 16-3 cannot exceed ____ feet.

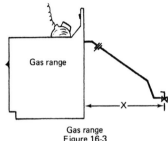

Gas range
Figure 16-3

(A)   4
(B)   6

(C)   8
(D) 10

Standard Gas Code

Answer: B

Code response: All gas appliances shall have accessible gas shut-off valves located no further than 6 feet from the appliance.

16-24 Portable outdoor gas-fired appliances may be connected with gas hose connectors listed for that purpose. Length of hose "X" in Figure 16-4 must be no more than ____ feet, if it is to meet Code specifications.

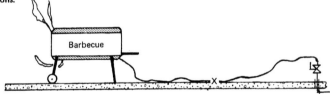

Barbecue
Figure 16-4

(A)   6
(B) 10

(C) 12
(D) 15

Standard Gas Code

Answer: D

Code response: The length of assembled connectors for portable outdoor gas-fired appliances shall be limited to 15 feet.

Plumbers should know how to install water heaters, ranges, dryers, and room heaters that are fueled by gas. This example from a page in a plumbers' exam preparation guide shows questions about a gas stove and a gas barbecue.

session, which lasts for six weeks. This extra class is a requirement for anyone wishing to enter the oil burner mechanic trade. An oil burner mechanic performs systems analysis, maintenance, inspections, and repairs on steam and hot water boilers, water heaters, and other hot water piping systems. At the end of the apprenticeship, the plumber will have complete knowledge of every aspect of plumbing.

In the classroom, the plumber-in-training learns drafting and blueprint reading, plumbing safety issues, and local plumbing regulations and codes. (The National Standard Plumbing Code [NSPC] sets standards for the installation, replacement, and repair of plumbing fixtures and pipes. Each state has its own plumbing code, and many counties and towns have their own codes, most of which are based on the NSPC's or on federal guidelines.) He or she also takes math classes and applied chemistry and physics classes. Then, when he or she is working in his or her apprenticeship, he or she will learn to identify, work with, and install various types and grades of pipe and piping systems and fixtures, and safely load and unload these and other materials.

PROFESSIONAL ASSOCIATIONS, ORGANIZATIONS, AND GROUPS

There are a number of organizations that a plumber may join. For example, there is the United Association of Plumbers and Pipefitters. This professional association has 321 local chapters from Florida to Washington State. The Web site for Local 598 in Pasco, Washington, says:

United Association [UA] Local 598 firmly believes that communication is important to its continued success and growth in today's competitive environment. Our commitment to providing superior quality products and cost effective services is key information that needs to be

HOW TO READ BLUEPRINTS/SYMBOLS AND FIGURES

Symbol		Description
——— — — — · —	C.W.	——— —— · — · — Cold water
——— ·· ——·· — · —	H.W.	——— ·· ——— ·· — Hot water
——— · ·· ——— · ·· —	H.W.R.	——— · · · ——— · · · — Hot water return
—————————	W.L.	————————— Waste line
— — — — — — — —	V.L.	— — — — — — — Vent line
—————————	S S	————————— Sanitary sewer
—————————	C	————————— Condensate line
—————————	S D	————————— Storm drain
—————————	R.W.L.	————————— Rain water leader
—→—→—→	I.W.	—→—→— Indirect waste
—————————	F	————————— Fire line
—————————	G	————————— Gas line
———▷◁———		————————— Gate valve
———▷●◁———		————————— Globe valve
———▷⊢———		————————— Check valve
—————————	R	————————— Relief line
		————————— P&T relief valve
———⊗— F.C.O.		——— Floor cleanout
⦿ F.D.		Floor drain
⦿ P.D.		Planter drain
⊘ R.D.		Roof drain
—•—⊢— H.B.		Hose bibb
⦿ A.D.		Area drain

These are the standard symbols and figures that a plumber needs to know to be able to read blueprints. The symbols depict a variety of water and waste lines, valves, and drains.

conveyed. This commitment is supported by all levels of management, from the Local to the International levels of UA organization, and is achieved through the productivity and excellence of our highly skilled union members. It follows that it is important to relay this commitment not only to our clientele, but also to the UA membership and prospective apprentices.

The Board of State Examiners of Plumbers and Gas Fitters, located in Boston, for example, is responsible for the regulation of plumbers and gas fitters in the Commonwealth of Massachusetts.

The Board of State Examiners of Plumbers and Gas Fitters is responsible for holding exams for journeymen and master plumbers. It also issues licenses for journeymen and master plumbers. It takes care of registering the apprentice plumbers and issuing plumbers their corporate and partnership certificates for plumbing. In addition, the board holds public hearings for the purpose of discussing code amendments, as well as the granting of variances and the approval of dual and elevated gases and plumbing and gas products. Also according to the Local 598 site:

The Board of State Examiners of Plumbers and Gas Fitters licenses approximately 23,579 plumbers and gas fitters in the Commonwealth. In fiscal year 2003, Board investigators inspected 642 premises, checking 588 licenses. The Board received 118 new complaints and resolved 260 complaints from this and previous fiscal years. The Board held one investigative conference, entered into one consent agreement, revoked 28 licenses, suspended 58 licenses and issued three stayed suspensions and one reprimand. The Board facilitated the refund of $9,278 in total.

According to the U.S. Department of Labor Veterans' Employment and Training Service, the American Society of Plumbing Engineers (ASPE) provides plumbers with a service whereby they can become certified as plumbers. They have a Certified in Plumbing Engineering (CIPE) certification, which was created for the purpose of providing professional recognition of those people who "design plumbing systems, provide a standard of professional competence in the practice of plumbing engineering, and enhance the status of plumbing engineering as a unique discipline and profession by clearly defining a realistic standard of professional competence."

While there is no one uniform set of requirements for national licensing, most areas of the United States require their plumbers to be licensed. However, requirements for these licenses will be different to some degree depending on where you live. Plumbers are typically required to pass an exam that tests not only their knowledge of plumbing in general but also their knowledge of the local plumbing codes. Some states have adopted the Universal Plumbing Code (UPC). In these states, plumbers are also required to pass a test of their knowledge of the UPC. Most states require all apprentices to be registered and all plumbers to be licensed.

In order to get a journeyman license, a plumber must have proof of two to four years of work experience under the supervision of a journeyman or master plumber. To obtain a master plumber license, a plumber needs to complete a specified number of years or hours of practical plumbing experience, must already have a license as a journeyman, and must pass an exam as well. Some areas also require their plumbers to join the local chapter of the union. While the licensing requirements vary from state to state, some states have agreements of reciprocity whereby plumbers who have licenses from other states may use these licenses in those states. It is necessary, however, to contact your own state directly for the specific requirements.

Other organizations for plumbers include the American Society of Sanitary Engineering (ASSE), whose members include plumbers from all segments of the plumbing industry. The group holds an annual meeting, which includes a two-day seminar. Attending this meeting and seminar benefits plumbers, helping them to stay on top of the latest industry trends. New information regarding services, products, research, codes, and legislation are presented along with a panel discussion on a specific hot topic. In addition, membership in this society allows plumbers to communicate and network with other plumbers as well as other member construction workers throughout the industry. The society provides lists of timely publications to its members. With chapters in twenty states, dues are kept manageable so that anyone from a student to a retired plumber can afford to join.

The ASSE Web site lists membership, chapter, and national benefits, and technical and special activities, which will give you an idea of how it will benefit you as a plumber to belong to an organization such as this one. These are some of the privileges given to members:

- Belonging to an organization represented by all segments of the industry, forming a platform to receive, understand, and solve industry problems relating to code, contracting, engineering, sales, and business
- Immediate voting rights for all active, life, and honorary members at national and chapter meetings
- Reduced fees for student/apprentice members
- Reduced membership for retired members with less than twenty-five years of membership
- Life membership for retired members with twenty-five years or more of membership
- Achievement recognition awards: Henry B. Davis (highest honor); honorary (non-member); fellow (exemplary service); and twenty-five, thirty-five, and fifty-year membership awards

The ASSE's national benefits include:

- Receiving monthly international newsletter containing society news and activities, and quarterly magazine, *Plumbing Standards*, containing technical articles, code and standards information, and industry updates
- Receiving the annual meeting yearbooks of the business and refresher course technical programs
- Receiving discounts on all society publications
- Attending annual meeting. Registration benefits include the refresher course; trade shows; business session with committee reports, chapter reports, and elections; and dinner dance and other social functions
- Participation in National Committee activity

Members' chapter benefits include the following:

- Attending chapter meetings, technical programs, field trips, sports outings, etc.
- Serving on chapter committees of special interest and receiving chapter publications, awards, etc.

The United Association of Journeymen and Apprentices of the Plumbing, Pipefitting, Sprinkler Fitting Industry of the United States and Canada's motto is: "The person who works with his hands is a laborer; the person who works with his hands and his head is an artisan; the person who works with his hands, his head, and his heart is a member of the UA." This association is more than 100 years old and, as of 2004, has a membership that exceeds 300,000 industry workers.

A MASTER PLUMBER FINDING A PERFECT CAREER

Randy Chalfant, thirty-six, of Webster City, Iowa, is the owner of Chalfant Plumbing, Heating, and Air Conditioning. But before he became a business owner, Chalfant worked as a plumber for eight years. He had this to say about his career:

I have several job titles right now. I am a master plumber, a heating and air-conditioning technician, and a business owner. I have owned my own business, Chalfant Plumbing, Heating, and Air Conditioning, for seven years. Before that, I was a plumber for another plumbing firm in my town. I was a residential plumber, which means I only worked in homes. I never did any of the industrial or commercial plumbing. In this community, that is all there is, just the residential work. I live in a fairly small town.

My primary responsibilities were the repair and servicing of existing plumbing. I replaced water lines and drains, repaired leaky pipes, replaced fixtures, and cleaned out drains. I would say I was also responsible for the one-on-one communication with our clients. That firm I was working for had a secretary who made all of our appointments and such, but when I went out on a job, it was my responsibility to make the contact with the customers when I got to their homes. I had to work with them to figure out exactly what the problem was so that I could tell them exactly what I would be doing to fix it.

As far as the future is concerned, if you are a service plumber, there is always going to be work for you. There are always going to be repairs needed. Right now I am working on new construction, which in this area is good. I have read that there are many plumbers working on new construction in most places. So, I would have to say that the future is good for the new plumber.

The main qualification or requirement needed for the job I had was that I had to have two years' experience working for a licensed plumber before I could take the test to get my license to become a journeyman plumber. At least that is how it is here in Webster City. So, basically I had to do an apprenticeship. Here in Webster City, the requirement to take the test to become a master plumber is four years of apprenticeship, that is to say, that you have to do the first two years, then take the journeyman test, and then do another two years and then take the master test. The difference between a journeyman and a master is that a journeyman's license allows you to do the work, while a master's license allows you to own your own business. In some parts of the country, you can go straight for your master's [license], but that varies from place to place.

I did not go to school to become a plumber. I was raised on a farm. Farming was what I thought I would always do. After I graduated high school, I moved to Houston, Texas, without a job. I met a guy in my apartment building right away and he told me that they could use some more plumbers out on the job. I had never thought of plumbing work before that, but I needed a job and money, so I looked into it. I never dreamed that one day here I would be, owner of my own plumbing company. But I knew pretty early on after I got started that I wanted to have my own shop one day.

I got most of my training on the job. There was just the boss and one other guy and me. When I was finished with my apprenticeship, I had to take a test to get my license. Most of the time, the employer will pay the fee for you to take your test. It's about $50. The test actually has two parts: a written exam and a hands-on, practical portion.

So now I have my master plumbing license. I do not belong to a union. There is no union here in Webster City, which is part of the reason why I do not belong to one. The other reason is that I just do not feel that residential plumbers really need to belong to a union. When I think union, I think commercial work.

When asked what personal qualifications one should bring to this job, Chalfant says:

Good communication skills, good common sense, and a good work ethic. You work by yourself a lot, and if you do not have a good work ethic, if you just sit around on a bucket for two hours sleeping, you are not going to get your job done. You have to want to get up and go to work and do something each day. You have to be self-motivated. Otherwise you will not get any work done, so you will not make any money, and then you will get fired.

If you are looking for an apprenticeship, there are really two ways you can go about getting one. You can do what I did, which is basically calling up a place or going there and asking for a job. I had heard that this guy was looking to hire someone. So I called him up and went in for a regular interview with the father, who was actually already retired, and his sons, who were running the business. The other way to get an apprenticeship is to join a union and get into their apprenticeship. In the bigger cities, this is usually the way it is done. You can just look in your phone book for the nearest union hall and give them a call. You will tell them that you are interested in becoming a plumber and you want to know about their apprenticeship program. You will want to find out exactly what they have available and when. The apprenticeship programs only take people at certain times during the year. You may have to take an aptitude test just to get into the apprenticeship. Also, you will need your high school diploma and you will have to be at least eighteen years old. The union hall apprenticeships are five years long and include school every other Saturday for training in addition to your nine-to-five workweek. Once you are in your apprenticeship, you will learn all of the tricks of the trade, from how to put pipes together and solder them, to how to repair toilets and faucets, to how to clear drains, to the brands of things. You will also learn about the plumbing codes. You will work on about four or five houses a year (if you are working in new construction), and you will need to know what you can and cannot do. During your apprenticeship, you will also learn about customer service, like how to deal with the different customers. While on the job, you will learn all about your different customers and their quirks. You will learn how to have a good conversation with them, and you will also learn to read them. For example, you will learn which customers will call only when there is a true emergency and which customers consider everything to be an emergency!

My typical work environment is someone's house. Usually my workday was from 8:00 in the morning until 5:00 in the evening, during which time I went to six or seven houses and did repairs and then moved on to the next house.

Here in this area, a working plumber can make from $25,000 a year on the low end, up to about $75,000. An owner can make from $75,000 to a high end of $100,000 in a small town. The average union scale currently is $28 to $30 an hour for a journeyman, which comes to about $62,000 a year.

If you are thinking about plumbing as a career, I will tell you that you can make a good career of this if you are good with your hands and willing to work with your hands. This is a career in which you get dirty, but it is worth it because you can make good money. The work is unlimited. If you wanted to work twenty-four hours a day, the work is there, someone is always calling.

I own my own business now. Why? Because the money is good and I wanted to be able to be more flexible with my work time. I have three full-time employees. We still do residential plumbing, plus we do heating and air conditioning work as well. Yes, you can definitely make a good career for yourself in the plumbing trade.

AND WHAT ABOUT THE FUTURE?

Work for plumbers is good now, and the expectation is that the opportunities within the industry will continue to grow steadily along with the average for all other construction jobs. While plumbers may find enough work on short-term construction jobs, they will have an even better time finding steadier work if they look for maintenance, renovation, and repair work. According to Paul Phifer in *Great Careers in 2 Years*, "Employment opportunities fluctuate with local economic conditions, although the plumbing industry is less affected by economic trends than other construction trades."

CHAPTER 4

MASON

Masons build or work with stone, brick, or cement. The term "mason" is a blanket term that covers a broad spectrum of more specific job titles. For example, you may decide to become a brick and block mason, a stonemason, or a concrete mason, all of which have varied job expectations and responsibilities. However, the masonry industry offers a wide range of different career opportunities.

WHAT MASONS DO

In the Vocational Information Center's Masonry Career Guide, a career and technical online resource created and maintained by Kathryn Hake, the following job titles fall under the description of a mason:

- Apprentice bricklayers
- Apprentice cement masons
- Architecture and construction careers
- Brick and block masons
- Brick masons

- Bricklayers
- Building contractors
- Building site managers
- Cement masons
- Concrete finishers
- Concrete and terrazzo finishers
- Concrete masons and terrazzo workers
- Concrete workers
- Construction and building inspectors
- Construction contractors and supervisors
- Construction technologists
- Construction trade helpers
- Construction managers
- Helpers—brick, block tile
- Paving machine operators
- Plasterers and stucco masons
- Reinforcing iron and rebar workers (These workers position and fasten the steel bars or mesh that is used in concrete forms.)
- Skilled trades, technology, and manufacturing
- Structural drafters (A structural drafter serves as the link between the structural engineer and the construction worker by preparing and producing technical drawings applying industry standards and regulations, performing necessary calculations, and doing appropriate research before creating his or her designs. Using technical terms, the drawings explain the details of the structure, the specific materials that will be used, and the procedures to be used. In addition, the structural drafter writes up a technical report, which includes an estimate of the project's cost.)
- Stonemason
- Tiler—wall and floor
- Tile setters
- Trade helpers and laborers

That's quite a few options to consider if you are thinking of becoming a mason!

While each of these options cannot be individually investigated in a book of this size, you will come away from this chapter with a good idea of what you might look forward to doing should you choose a career as a mason.

WHAT IS A MASON?

A mason is a skilled artist who works with his or her hands, as well as with hand tools, power tools, and material-moving equipment, to turn brick, tile, stone, concrete block, glass block, and terra-cotta into structures as simple as a wall to those as complex as a high-rise building. The trade is diverse in its opportunities.

As a mason, you will know how to read blueprints and understand building codes as well as the guidelines for handling the various hazardous materials (such as silica, a hazardous substance in large quantities, which is used in concrete and mortar mixes) that you will find on the job. Also, you may be qualified to work at different levels, all the way up to a management position. Among the positions you may hold, according to Masonry-Training.com, are the following:

- Estimator
- Job-site supervisor or foreman
- Mason contractor
- Masonry instructor
- Project manager
- Quality control technician (the person who does final testing on the work that has been done to ensure that all aspects of the project have been done properly and accurately and to safety code standards)
- Superintendent

You may be required to seek further training to specialize in some of these areas. As you may have already figured out, the term "mason" is a blanket title that covers a lot of specialized jobs. Let us take a look at some of these specific jobs that make up the entire field of masonry.

BRICK AND BLOCK MASONS

These masons are responsible for laying and binding building materials. These materials can be bricks, concrete blocks, cinder blocks, structural tile, glass blocks, and terra-cotta blocks. They use mortar to construct or to repair various structures ranging from walls and partitions to arches and sewers. According to Career Zone (a free career research Web site at http://www.nycareerzone.org that is sponsored by New York State and that combines career and labor market information), the specific tasks required of the brick and block mason are:

- Mixing specified amounts of sand, clay, dirt, or mortar powder with water to form refractory mixture (a mixture that can endure high temperatures, such as those used in brick ovens and kilns)
- Calculating angles and courses and determining vertical and horizontal alignment of courses
- Laying and aligning bricks, blocks, or tiles to build or repair structures or high temperature equipment, such as cupolas, kilns, ovens, or furnaces
- Applying and smoothing mortar or other mixture over work surfaces and removing excess, using trowels and hand tools
- Examining brickwork or structure to determine need for repair
- Measuring distance from reference points and marking guidelines to lay out work, using plumb bobs and levels

- Breaking or cutting bricks, tiles, or blocks to size, using edge of trowel, hammer, or power saw
- Removing burned or damaged brick or mortar, using sledgehammer, crowbar, chipping gun, or chisel
- Spraying or spreading refractory material over brickwork to protect against deterioration
- Cleaning working surface to remove scale, dust, soot, or chips of brick and mortar, using broom, wire brush, or scraper
- Fastening or fusing brick or other building material to structure with wire clamps, anchor holes, torch, or cement

As you might realize from reading the above list, a number of different skills are involved in the work of a mason. His or her skills will range from practical personal skills to factual skills. For example, the mason should be good with math as he or she will need mathematical skills to solve work-related problems. He or she will be responsible for choosing the proper equipment and tools with which he or she will do his or her work. He or she will also be expected to monitor and assess his or her own performance by taking measurements to be sure the work is even and level, and by using his or her keen eye to check that the job is done correctly. He or she will need to know how to repair the machines and systems, such as a concrete mixer, that are used on the job. He or she will need to know how to install machines, equipment, and wiring to meet certain standard specifications. He or she will also need a great deal of knowledge about his or her trade. According to Career Zone, a mason needs knowledge in several different areas.

He or she will need to have a working knowledge of the materials, methods, and tools used in building and constructing homes, buildings, and roadways, as well as those used in repairs and maintenance. His or her mathematical skills should include a substantial background in arithmetic, algebra, geometry, calculus, and statistics, as well as physics. He or she will need to be proficient in the areas of engineering and technology, specifically in the application of principles, techniques, procedures, and equipment used to do the work. He or she will also need to be able to properly use the design tools, understand the design techniques and principles, and be able to read and understand blueprints, drawings, and models. And, above all, he or she needs to be fluent in reading, writing, speaking, and understanding the English language.

To do the work of a brick or block mason, you will need an education that includes training from a vocational school and some related on-the-job experience. You may need an associate's degree or even a bachelor's degree depending on where you work and what your aspirations are within the trade.

What's the Pay?

It is all worth the time and effort. According to Career Zone, the annual wage range for a block or brick mason working in New York in 2002 was $38,784 to $66,977. "This range represents the middle 50% of workers. Some (25%) earned more than this, while others (25%) earned less," according to Career Zone.

The Stonemason

Stonemasonry is another type of masonry to consider as a possible area for a career. Stonemasons are skilled artisans who build structures such as exterior and interior walls, floors, fireplaces, and chimneys. They work with two types of stone. One type is natural cut stone. Natural cut stone includes granite, marble, and sandstone. The other type of stone is artificial. Artificial stone can be stone made from marble chips, cement, and various other masonry materials. A stone mason may be responsible for any or even all of the following:

- Aligning stones with plumb line
- Attaching brackets and welding them to anchors
- Cleaning finished surface of stones
- Pouring footings
- Removing wedges and "tuck" point (Tuck pointing is a process by which deteriorated mortar is removed from the joints of a masonry and replaced with new mortar for the purpose of restoring both the visual and the physical integrity of the masonry.)
- Setting stone in place by hand or with a crane
- Shaping stones prior to setting
- Spreading mortar over foundations and stones

WORKING CONDITIONS OF THE STONEMASON

If you consider yourself an outdoor person who is willing to brave the elements, perhaps a career in stonemasonry is right for you. However, despite your willingness to work in all weather, most stonemasonry jobs depend on good weather. A good stonemason is physically fit to fulfill the required tasks of the job, such as lifting and carrying heavy materials and supplies, as well as standing, kneeling, and bending for lengthy periods of time. The greatest hazard of the job is injury from tools or from falling off scaffolding. Stonemasons can generally expect to work a standard forty-hour workweek, with occasional overtime when a deadline must be met. Twenty-five percent of all stonemasons are self-employed.

Unlike some of the other trades you are reading about in this book, the stonemason is not required to sit through several years of school and apprenticeships before becoming gainfully employed. In fact, although there are formal training centers around the country, usually found in community colleges, most stonemasons are trained informally by professional stonemasons. This on-the-job training often takes more time than an apprenticeship would, lasting up to four years, as opposed to the average three years of on-the-job training offered in apprenticeships. The would-be mason usually begins his or her on-the-job training as one of three different types of workers: a helper, a laborer, or a mason tender. At this level, he or she performs such tasks as mixing mortar, carrying the materials used on the job, and moving scaffolding. As time goes by, he or she will have an opportunity to learn how to spread mortar, lay blocks and bricks, and set stones. Eventually, with enough experience, he or she will become a craftworker.

If you wish to obtain the formal training to become a stonemason, you can expect a training curriculum to include courses in masonry techniques, such as in tool selection, stone selection, foundation pouring, and stone shaping. The average course takes one year to complete. Also, unlike some of the other trades in this book, there is no training through the armed forces available for the would-be stonemason.

THE STONEMASON OF THE FUTURE

One area in which there is similarity between stonemasons and other construction tradesmen is the outlook for the future. The prospects of stonemasons are as bright as those for other careers. While an enormous need for new stonemasons is not expected, the need will continue to rise at a modest rate as long as both the population and the businesses of the United States continue to grow and require an increase in the construction of schools, hospitals, office buildings, and factory buildings.

WHAT'S THE PAY?

The average starting salary for a stonemason ranges from $24,960 to $27,690. The average salary range for an experienced stonemason ranges from $38,845 to $47,475.

CEMENT MASONS

Yet another type of mason is the cement mason. Concrete is a popular, useful, and durable material, so it is commonly used in all sorts of building projects. It is usually used to make the foundation of various structures, such as floors, patios, and even roads. The cement mason is the person who places and finishes concrete for all sorts of different construction jobs.

He or she starts by preparing the work site. This is done by setting up forms to hold the concrete in the proper depth and pitch (how deep and wide the area will be). Then he or she directs the pouring of the concrete, which is called casting. He or she oversees the workers who are charged with spreading the cement with their tools, such as shovels. The cement mason steps up to level the concrete and smooth the surface before finishing the concrete.

The concrete finishers work to round the edges, which helps to prevent the concrete from cracking and chipping later on. Using a groover, he or she marks grooves at specific intervals, which also helps to stop the concrete from cracking when it is set and dry. Then, using a trowel, he or she finishes the surface. The cement mason then trowels the surface one more time to give it a smooth finish. However, if the surface is meant to be coarse, the mason will brush the surface with a stiff brush before it dries. Even more finishing is needed for surfaces that will remain exposed following the removal of the forms, such as ceilings and columns.

The cement mason then cuts away any loose concrete with a hammer and chisel and fills large dents with cement paste, then smoothes the surface with an abrasive rubbing stone. The final layer is a rich cement mixture, which coats the layers beneath it and is then rubbed with a coarse cloth for a finish that is uniform.

While all of this is being done, the cement mason must carefully watch the concrete to see what it is doing relative to heat, cold, and wind. The cement mason uses his or her senses of touch and sight to find out what the concrete is doing in order to take proper measures to avoid defects in the work.

In addition to the specific tasks you just read about, Internet System for Education and Knowledge (http://www.Iseek.org), a Minnesota career information Web site, lists a number of a cement mason's tasks. These include controlling machines and processes, obtaining the required information to do the job, handling and moving objects such as equipment for the job, inspecting equipment to be sure it is in proper working order, and inspecting structures for proper building technique or flaws and materials to be sure they are the right ones for the job and in good working order. He or she will have to determine the value of services rendered. He or she will need to watch the other workers on the job site, keep an eye on the materials to be sure they are appropriate, and check out the surroundings for safety reasons. He or she will have to be strong and agile as use of the entire body is common in this trade.

Working Conditions

There are many different aspects you can expect to find regarding working conditions if you become a concrete mason. You can expect to work a regular forty-hour workweek. For the majority of those hours, you will be working alone with little or no interaction with others. In terms of your physical self, the working conditions vary but can often be rather unpleasant. While you may work on some jobs that allow you to be inside, most of your jobs will take place outside, so you must be prepared to work in extreme cold and heat to get your job done. You may be required to wear protective gear such as kneepads or water-repellent boots, depending on the job, because you may be exposed to contaminants, such as the chemicals from uncured concrete.

You will want to pay close attention to the details of your work. After all, even a minor error could cause you to have to redo the entire project. You will be using your body in the same range of movements over and over again to get your work done. You will use your hands to handle and operate tools and controls, and stand on your feet for long periods of time. You must be able to comfortably kneel and crawl, and bend or twist to reach your work and perform it properly. Be ready to repeat these motions again and again. And although you may want to work more quickly or slowly at any given time, you will often have to work along with the pace of the machinery with which you are working. As you can see, this is the kind of job best suited to a person in good physical condition, both in terms of fine and gross motor abilities as well as in stamina. In addition, you must be able to speak plainly so your instructions are clearly understood, and you should understand written instructions and information. And you must also have good eyesight to see objects in glaring or very bright light and also be able to easily determine the distance between objects.

Strong math skills will help you solve problems on the job, and strong problem-solving skills will help you identify and analyze problems and make appropriate changes to get the job done properly. The ability to imagine how something will look if it is rearranged is important to this job as well.

What does it take to actually get a job? While you will not need much if any previous work experience, you will be required to supply proof of a high school diploma or a GED. Most employers prefer high school graduates. If you are considering a formal education to become a concrete mason, you can expect to spend between three and five years in your apprenticeship, during which time you will receive 144 hours of classroom training in addition to on-the-job-training. In the classroom, you will study mathematics, blueprint reading, and important safety practices. While doing on-the-job training, you will learn how to mix and pour concrete; use materials, tools, and equipment; trowel; and lay blocks. Training is also available through professional technical schools or two-year colleges. However, as previously mentioned, the majority of cement masons learn their skills informally on the job. To prepare for your career this way, you may start as a helper on the job, gaining experience and skills from an experienced worker. This type of training may also last for several years.

While you are still in high school, work toward earning your high school diploma. As mentioned already, you will need this to get a job. You can begin to prepare by taking such classes as math, science, social studies, English, physical education, health, applied art, and foreign language. You may also wish to consider taking an introductory course in business. Construction trades classes, such as construction, exploration of construction careers, construction trades work experience, and masonry, if they are available, would also be helpful. Drafting classes and blueprint reading classes will come in handy. A course in safety and first aid is also a good one to take.

When considering which math classes to take, think about general math, applied math, pre-algebra and algebra, business math, and integrated math classes. You should also consider taking classes such as driver's education, an exploratory of careers class, general industrial arts, and industrial and technology work experience classes. To prepare for the physical side of the job, it would be smart to take both physical education and fitness and conditioning classes. Taking this last set of classes will be to your advantage, especially if your future employer requires you to submit to a physical exam before beginning your new job.

FACTS AND NUMBERS

First, you may find it interesting to note that a cement mason does not need a license or a certificate of any sort to work on a job. So, now let's talk cash. How much money will you make working as a cement mason?

According to the Department of Labor's Bureau of Labor Statistics May 2003 national estimates, the national average pay is $16.23 per hour, with half of all cement masons earning about $33,760.

The wages also depend on the cement mason's experience. Bad weather can bring the total down because it is often the cause for loss of work. Another factor to consider is that cement masons may suffer from lack of work when the economy is slow. Your benefits package will also vary depending on whom you are working for and where. Along with three other related trades (concrete finishers, segmental pavers, and terrazzo workers), cement masons held approximately 190,000 jobs in 2002. Most cement masons are employed by concrete contractors or general contractors. They work on projects such as bridges, highways, malls, and large buildings. A smaller percentage of cement masons work for firms that manufacture various concrete products. A mere one in twenty cement masons is self-employed, but those who are tend to specialize in smaller jobs, for example, patios, sidewalks, and driveways, according to the U.S. Department of Labor.

A BRIGHT FUTURE

The future demand for those who work in the masonry industry is bright. The national expectation, according to Iseek.org, is that there will be a slow but steady increase in the need for

National Estimates for Cement Masons and Concrete Finishers as Reported in May 2003 by the U.S. Department of Labor, Bureau of Labor Statistics

Employment estimate and mean wage estimates for this occupation:

Employment (1)	Employment RSE (3)	Mean hourly wage	Mean annual wage (2)	Wage RSE (3)
180,540	2.3 %	$16.23	$33,760	0.8 %

Percentile wage estimates for this occupation:

Percentile	10%	25%	50% (Median)	75%	90%
Hourly Wage	$10.04	$12.66	$16.47	$21.85	$28.00
Annual Wage (2)	$20,890	$26,330	$34,250	$45,440	$58,240

1. Estimates for detailed occupations do not sum to the totals because the totals include occupations not shown separately. Estimates do not include self-employed workers.
2. Annual wages have been calculated by multiplying the hourly mean wage by a year-round, full-time hours figure of 2,080 hours.
3. The relative standard error (RSE) is a measure of the reliability of a survey statistic. The smaller the relative standard error, the more precise the estimate.

masons through 2010. Slow may not sound like a buzz word to listen for, but the phrase "is expected to grow" is key even if the expectation does not exceed that which was seen in the past.

Let's take a look at the reality of the industry. One reason this industry is expecting a less than average growth over the next five or so years is because of the expected increase in individual workers' productivity, due to improved machinery, equipment, and tools. However, Iseek.org reassures future masons that "despite the slow growth, opportunities for skilled cement masons will be good." This is because a continued increase in demand for work to be done will outpace the population of trained masons. Also, as long as there are masons, there will be retiring masons. So, for every mason who retires, a spot opens up for a new mason to take his or her place.

Of course, if you look at the average employment of the average given mason, you may still find some periods of unemployment because the nature of many mason jobs is short-term and considered cyclical (that is, the jobs can be dependent on the economy, the housing market, and even on the season, and there can be a decrease in demand for masons during the cold winter months). When the economy is slow, job opportunities for masons will be less plentiful than average. Of course, there is always the potential for growth within the industry, so if you are wary of the economy and your potential as a mason, you should keep in mind that there is always potential for growth. If you set your sights higher, you may be able to work your way up to becoming a contract estimator or a supervisor, or perhaps even the owner of your own masonry company.

According to the Web site Internet System for Education and Knowledge (Iseek.org), the number of job openings for cement masons is expected to grow about 3 percent from 2000 to 2010. In 2000, there were 162,500 jobs nationally for cement masons, whereas in 2010 the estimated number will be 167,400 jobs.

MASONRY SCHOOL

As with the other trades you have read about in this book, spending time as an apprentice and taking approved courses to become a mason are options. If you join other apprentice programs, you can expect to spend between two and four years both in the classroom and gaining experience on the job. "While tuition is usually charged for training, apprentices can 'earn while they learn' at a rate of 50% to 90% of journeyman wages during their 'on-the-job' training. Also, employing contractors often cover most apprentices' tuition," according to the National Concrete Masonry Association (NCMA) Web site.

MASONING FOR MONEY

According to the NCMA Web site, a mason is one of the highest-paid skilled workers in the construction trades. In fact, it is not unusual for a bricklayer to take home a higher wage than a college graduate. Of course, how much money you actually make will depend on the area in which you are working, as well as the employer for whom you are working. You may be surprised to learn that in addition to the great pay you will receive for your work as a mason, you will also be eligible for some terrific benefits. "Most mason contractors are competitive when it comes to providing benefits for their employees. Bricklayers often receive health and dental insurance, vacation and sick leave, a 401K or other retirement plan and other benefits," says the NCMA Web site.

The future looks good for those thinking about a career as a mason. In fact, in recent years, there has been a reported shortage of masons. The U.S. Department of

Labor reports that by 2005, masons will be among a shortage of 1 million skilled workers in the construction industry. The United States Bureau of Labor Statistics is estimating that by 2005, approximately 800,000 new jobs will be created in the construction trades. But the brightest star in the future of masonry, according to the NCMA, is that "the skills of a mason can never be replaced by machine." This means that a well-trained mason has a bright and lucrative career ahead of him or her.

BECOMING PART OF THE GROUP: ORGANIZATIONS

Like the other trades you are reading about in this book, masonry is a trade that also has its own organizations and groups that you can join.

The National Concrete Masonry Association (NCMA) is one of these organizations. Established in 1918, the NCMA is the national trade association that represents the concrete masonry industry. According to its own Web site, the NCMA "is involved in a broad range of technical, research, marketing, government relations, and communications activities. NCMA is an association of producers of concrete masonry products, and suppliers of products and services related to the industry. NCMA offers a variety of technical services and design aids through publications, computer programs, slide presentations and technical training."

A VIEWPOINT ABOUT A CAREER AS A MASON

In early 2004, Terry Mulligan (from a suburb of Chicago, Illinois) retired from a long, satisfying, and lucrative career as a mason. He looks back fondly on his work with no regrets for the years he spent working with his hands.

I was president and CEO of my own company. We started out in 1973 with just $1,500, a used pickup truck, and a used mixer. By the time I retired, we were doing nearly $10,000,000 a year. I loved my work, absolutely loved it. But I'd had some health problems, and one day I just got up and went to the work site, took a look at the huge job in front of me, and said, "That's it. I've had enough." And I retired on the spot. People don't do that too often, but I just felt I'd given this career my all and now I was finished. It was a truly wonderful career and I just loved my work!

When I was in high school, I worked for a road construction company. The labor laws were different then. You had to be sixteen to do this work, but I lied and got my work permit. Today, I think you have to be eighteen or maybe even twenty-one to work construction. After high school, I did some work that was totally unrelated to construction, but by 1957, I was back on a road construction crew. I worked as a common laborer until I got my badge. Jobs were scarce then because you couldn't work in the winter when there was no shelter from the elements. So I was working maybe seven months out of the year and then filing for unemployment for the rest of the year.

I was working as a cement finisher, pouring basements and garage floors, sidewalks, and driveways. When you pour cement, you have to sit and wait for things to dry. I was sitting aside watching a bricklayer build a fireplace one day, and I just fell in love with what I saw. I had to become a bricklayer. I got permission from the unions to switch trades and then I got hired on by a contractor so I could get trained. I never went to school for any of this. I learned on the job. At twenty-nine years old, I realized that I wasn't going to go anywhere as a cement finisher. I had high aspirations, I was ambitious, and I knew I wanted to go places. So I did an on-the-job apprenticeship. Apprenticeships back in the 1950s were just emerging, so they were not like the apprenticeships of *today. It took me three years to get my journeyman's card so I could work. Business has always come naturally for me, and I had a vision of buying and renovating old buildings. Pretty quickly after I got my journeyman's card, I went into business for myself. I had forty men working for me right away. We had many major jobs. I had dreams of conquering the world.*

Masonry is probably the toughest [and] most physically demanding of all the trades because you have to lift your own equipment and materials, which are really heavy. So you have to be strong and physically fit to do this line of work. I don't think construction workers get enough respect for the work we do. We really work very hard out there. I was very proud of every job we did. I would just stand back and look at the finished buildings and I loved the beauty of them. I loved what we had created. My company won some awards for our work: Best Craftsman Award and Best Stone Job, both in the Northern Illinois and Indiana division. We did a lot of tricky jobs. I loved my work, the jobs we did, all we accomplished.

I think I have worked every facet of construction over the fifty-year period that I was in the workforce. I loved it all. For someone just thinking about becoming a mason, I would recommend he come out and work for a mason doing labor for about two years. Learn everything, especially the safety aspects and the various rules. Then decide. And if you are smart, you will learn everything there is to know. That way, when you are on a job, if someone calls in sick, you can jump right in and fill the sick guy's shoes. You will always be employed if you can do any and every aspect of a job. It's hard work, but if you can do it, if you can get in with the others and let them show you how to do things rather than trying to be the smartest guy on the job the very first day, your future will be secure.

A mason makes about $31 an hour plus benefits. You have to work 1,600 hours to have money contributed into your pension fund. At 1,600 hours, you are talking about a salary of about $48,000 a year. But most masons do the extra work and work about 2,000 hours, which brings in more like $60,000 a year. You can make up to about $80,000, and if you become foreman, you will make even a few dollars more an hour.

When I was hiring masons to work for me, we had to deal with the unions, so the laws say you can only ask questions so far about the guys you're hiring. I would just tell the union what I was looking for, skill-wise, and they would send me a qualified guy. They don't all have the same skills. I usually wanted a seasoned guy who could do everything: glass block, granite, brick, stone . . . Though the guys who had just gotten their union cards were usually quick, efficient, and energetic, too. To be a mason, in addition to having the strength of body, you also need to be good with your hands and have good eyesight so that you can tell if all of your work is level and accurate.

I don't have any sort of certificate or license. Illinois doesn't have a program like that. Some other states do, though. I belong to the Chamber of Commerce, the Greater Chicago Masonry Contractors Association, the Mason Contractors of Fox Valley, which just merged with the Chicago National MCAA. I was their legislative chairman for a few years. I lead groups to Washington, D.C., every year to talk to Congress about the needs of mason contractors.

There are not enough craftsmen to go around. We need new employees, and we need them to learn how to do the old ways of doing things so they can maintain and repair the work that was done years ago. I think there will be a lot of money in maintenance and repairs. It's really an untapped industry of its own. I think the future *of the mason is a good one. The trade will survive. Things are only getting better. Nowadays, you can work all year round since they will enclose the jobs in the winter now. Wages are going up, and now about $22,000 a year is put in for retirement, health, and annuity for each employee. There really are lots of opportunities to do this type of work.*

Go stand out in front of a church or a school that was built less than ten years ago. Now imagine yourself building this structure. Imagine the satisfaction you will feel when you can look at such a building and know that your hands made all of it possible. That is what my career was all about.

CHAPTER 5

TILER

Tilers install thin pieces of material, or tiles, made of plastic, stone concrete, or rubber, to cover roofs, walls, floors, and drains.

This chapter will cover what it means to be a tiler, what you need to do and know to become a tiler, and where to go for further information about apprenticeships and learning about tiling as a career.

WHAT DOES A WALL AND FLOOR TILER DO?

Simply put, a wall and floor tiler lays tiles. The tiles he or she works with may be made of ceramic, clay, glass, marble, slate, stone, or other materials. He or she may lay these tiles on internal or external walls and floors, on countertops, in bathrooms, in offices, in stores, in restaurants, and even in swimming pools. He or she will often do his or her work based on written, spoken, planned, or diagrammed instructions. But sometimes the tiler gets to design his or her own tile configuration. He or she will measure the area to be tiled and figure out how much of the materials are needed.

His or her job will be not only the laying of the tiles, however, but also the cutting of the tiles, as well as the preparing of the foundation on which the tiles will be laid. To prepare the foundation, the tiler may first remove old tiles. Whether this step is necessary depends on where he or she is working, as he or she may be working on a brand-new building in which no tiles currently exist. The tiler will level the surface and then prepare a suitable base for the tiles. This base may be made of sand and cement, plaster, or wood. After the base is prepared, the tiler can begin to lay the tiles. While most of the tiles will be laid as is, some tiles may require some cutting so that they will fit around pipes, appliances, openings, oddly shaped corners, or other spots that are not suitable for a standard tile. The tiler may be able to cut the tiles by hand or with a machine, depending on the tiles.

The tiles are then laid using an adhesive or a sand and cement mixture. Spaces, called joints, are left between the tiles. Later on, grout will be used to fill in the spaces. Neatness counts when you are laying tiles. If you do not place the tiles precisely and clean up the grout after you are finished, you will be left with a messy, uneven surface. The tiles, once in place, will provide finishes that are either decorative, protective, functional, or all of these.

So, You Want to Be a Tiler

There are two types of tiling that you will be thinking about here as you consider your tiling career: floor tiling and wall tiling. The industry of roof tiling is somewhat different and will be discussed only briefly in this book.

Working as a tiler is a great career choice if you like to work with your hands, have a good sense of artistry, and are adept with details and colors alike. Your work will be all hands-on as you create beautiful, durable walls and floors for homes, office and school buildings, store interiors, and other such structures.

An artistic eye will be a great advantage and is certainly somewhat of a necessity in this industry as you will be working to create patterns and both functional and artistic effects while you arrange tiles of different colors (or sometimes of the same color) and texture into various arrangements. Sometimes, your arrangements will be done in a mosaic style, other times you will do a straightforward laying of tiles. Either way, you must be able to pay very close attention to the details of your work. This is very exact and precise work, so if you have an eye for detail and a steady hand, a career in tiling may be right up your alley. Using your artistic abilities, you may find yourself tiling walls and floors in fancy mosaic patterns. To do this, you will arrange the various different-colored tiles in patterns specified by verbal or written instructions. The patterns may create specific designs, for example, flower or geometric patterns, such as three white tiles, one blue tile, three white tiles, and so on. Or you could be creating a freeform, abstract design that will still nonetheless have a set of instructions.

You may find yourself working on walls, floors, and even stairs, in all sorts of structures, such as homes, schools, factories, stores, restaurants, and offices. The materials you work with may vary as well. You may work with ceramic tiles and vinyl tiles, and you will learn how to lay sheet materials and carpets during your apprenticeship, which will make your skills that much more well-rounded.

Once you have decided that a career in tiling suits your artistic nature, you will consider completing a national certificate in floor and wall tiling. This will lead you to job opportunities.

WHAT SKILLS DO I NEED, EXACTLY?

Adaptability and flexibility are two of the key personality traits of the best tilers. There is a wide range when it comes to the different tiling tasks you may find yourself doing. In addition, you are also likely to find that you will need to know how to use a range of different materials. So, if you feel that you are good at adapting easily to new situations and that you are flexible in your abilities, you are heading in the right direction.

To become a tiler, perfectionism and a good visual sense are among the necessary personal traits that are recommended by most professional tilers. Other helpful attributes for this career are:

- Good eyesight
- Skill in working with your hands
- The ability to calculate, with precision, the number of tiles needed for a given job
- Being at least sixteen years old (although laws vary from state to state)
- Having good color vision (If you are color-blind or do not perceive colors well, you may have a hard time matching the colors of the materials used to make a perfect look.)

You should also possess these additional personal traits for a career as a tiler: You should be able to make simple calculations and work accurately, neatly, and independently. You should have no fear of working at high heights. You must be good with your hands. You should also have an interest in doing practical work.

The following skills are also important for a tiler: You will need to be able to carry out various tasks in a specific order. You must be willing and able to work alone at times and as part of a team at other times. You will need an aptitude for math because you will need to accurately measure and calculate the quantities of the materials you will need for your jobs. You should be able to plan your work carefully, methodically, and accurately. Creativity and an appreciation of design are important talents to possess when designing or matching tile patterns. You will need practical ability as well as excellent fine motor coordination to cut and lay the tiles. In addition, you must possess tact, flexibility, and a friendly attitude for dealing with clients.

What Should I Study in High School?

While there is no set curriculum that you will be required to follow while still in high school, there are some classes that come highly recommended to those looking into a career as a wall and floor tiler. Consider enrolling in courses that teach art, design, communications, crafts, English, and math.

Some of the core skills for potential wall and floor tilers include the following: communication skills, which include listening and speaking skills, particularly when explaining work details, aesthetic or artistic ideas, and instructions with supervisors and colleagues; computer skills, which include using computer graphics and design programs; number skills, which include mathematics skills for solving problems, taking measurements and calculating the number of tiles needed for a specific job, and reading and understanding blueprints, drawings, and diagrams of floors and walls; problem-solving skills, which include those for creating designs, matching patterns, imagining how something will look if it is rearranged, and determining the best methods, tools, and equipment for doing a particular job.

What Will I Be Doing, Exactly?

Once you have finished your apprenticeship, you will be armed with a number of skills that will take you through a good career. You will be able to accomplish a great number of tasks.

You will know how to look at plans, measure and mark the surface that you are going to work on, and lay out your tiling. You will know how to remove the old tiles, grout, cement, and adhesives so that you can prepare the wall and the floor surfaces for the new tiles. You will be skilled at filling holes and cracks, and you'll be able to clean your work surface properly.

In addition, you will be adept at using the correct adhesives to evenly space and attach tiles, ensuring that you are properly creating a pattern. You will know how to use your tile-cutting tools to cut and shape tiles to properly fit the design that you are working in, moving around pipes, corners, and edges cleanly. You will also know how to prepare, apply, and clean up grout, lay cement floors and terrazzo, and apply waterproofing to the finished product, ensuring its durability and longevity.

So, About That Apprenticeship . . .

Many states have apprenticeship programs that are run by trade schools or unions. Most tilers acquire their skills on the job by working as helpers for tilers who have experience. Voluntary certification in tile setting is available through trade groups, unions, and such organizations as the Ceramic Tile Institute of America, Inc. (CTIOA). For certification, the CTIOA requires the completion of thirty-two hours of classroom training (which includes taking tests at the end of each session), passing a four-hour written exam, and writing a 2,500-word research report. Some of the subjects taught at CTIOA include building code requirements that regulate tile installation, physical properties of ceramic and stone, installation specifications, setting materials specifications, marble tile installation, and installation of countertops, steam rooms, and ramps.

WORK CONDITIONS

As a wall and floor tiler, you are likely to find yourself working in a wide variety of locations and conditions. You may work some jobs inside already completed buildings and you may work some of your jobs outside as part of a construction team. You may, at times, find yourself working in small, confined, cramped spaces, in which you must kneel and bend frequently to get the job done. At other times, you will have to work high atop ladders or scaffolding.

Despite the fact that tilers work with their hands to create their work, tilers must also be physically fit, as they are required to lift and carry their own stacks of tiles and cement. You may also have to move furniture if you are working inside a home or office or other already occupied space. And, depending on the job, you may also have to rip out old tiling before putting in your beautiful new tiles. You can expect to work on a team with a couple of other tilers. Small jobs usually only require one tiler and often an apprentice. And you can plan on being flexible, because you will be moving from job to job, location to location.

HOW MUCH MONEY CAN I MAKE DOING THIS?

The chart on the facing page, which describes the income expectations for tilers and marble setters working full-time in 2003, was reported by the U.S. Department of Labor's Bureau of Labor Statistics. The average annual salary for tilers in 2003 was about $35,610. The wage range for the same year was $9.99 to $27.89 per hour.

JOINING PROFESSIONAL ORGANIZATIONS

Once you have become a professional floor and wall tiler, you should consider joining a professional organization, such as the National Tile Contractors Association

(NTCA). When you visit the NTCA's Web site (http://www.tile-assn.com), you will read about the organization, when and why it was created, and what benefits you will receive as a member.

National Estimates for Tile and Marble Setters as Reported in May 2003 by the U.S. Department of Labor, Bureau of Labor Statistics

Employment estimate and mean wage estimates for this occupation:

Employment (1)	Employment RSE (3)	Mean hourly wage	Mean annual wage (2)	Wage RSE (3)
36,900	5.0 %	$17.95	$37,340	1.6 %

Percentile wage estimates for this occupation:

Percentile	10%	25%	50% (Median)	75%	90%
Hourly Wage	$9.99	$12.72	$17.12	$22.08	$27.89
Annual Wage (2)	$20,780	$26,450	$35,610	$45,940	$58,010

1. Estimates for detailed occupations do not sum to the totals because the totals include occupations not shown separately. Estimates do not include self-employed workers.
2. Annual wages have been calculated by multiplying the hourly mean wage by a year-round, full-time hours figure of 2,080 hours.
3. The relative standard error (RSE) is a measure of the reliability of a survey statistic. The smaller the relative standard error, the more precise the estimate.

According to its Web site, "Organized and chartered in 1947, the National Tile Contractors Association (NTCA) is a non-profit trade association serving every segment of the industry, and is recognized as the largest and most respected national tile contractors association in the world."

The NTCA has a full staff, a board of elected officers, and committee members, all of whom are professionals in the trade. The NTCA works with its members on education, technology updates, and other issues within the industry. Its site also provides members with good resources related to the industry, such as reference manuals, trade magazines, books, videos, technical advice, an e-mail newsletter, workshops, and conferences, as well as an apprenticeship program.

You may also wish to consider membership in the Tile Contractors Association of America. This association, which celebrated its centennial in 2003, offers a vast array of resources to its members, ranging from technical training to legal assistance. This organization represents the tile contractors who are among the most well-respected for their work in the United States. The organization was founded in 1903 and is the only association that exclusively serves the needs of the tile contractor.

A Viewpoint About Being a Tile Setter

Jarrett Tatge is a forty-two-year-old self-employed tile setter from Brookfield, Illinois. The following is what he had to say about his career:

I'm a tiler, a wall and floor tiler. Really my title is tile setter. We set the tiles. Bricklayers and tile setters used to share the same union because we both use what is considered "hard goods," so we used to all be together.

I work for myself. My company is called Primarily Tile. I usually have just one or two other guys working with me. I have owned this company for twelve years. But I have been in the business for twenty-three years. Right after high school, I went to college, but only for a year. I was doing all sorts of odd jobs. One such job was at a White Hen Pantry [a convenience store]. One of my regular customers was a handyman, and he came in asking if I knew of anyone who wanted to make some extra money doing some part-time work with him. I wasn't satisfied with my current job status, so I told him I was interested. I spent four years with this handyman. I consider this time my training period. I did odd jobs for him, and then I started to learn to do the tile setting myself. It was slow going at first, but you get faster and more efficient and you learn to anticipate problems. So, after a few years, I started doing jobs for relatives and then for my friends' parents. Then I pretty much started working for myself right away, which I would not recommend. When you work for yourself, you are responsible for all the estimating and bidding and such. I recommend you get in with a company when you are first starting out. Get a taste of the job. In fact, I recommend you try this line of work even before you make any final decisions about whether or not you want to make a career of tile setting.

It's not for everyone. It's very physical, very hard on your body. There is the possibility of physical injury from the tools and even from some of the tiles themselves, such as the ceramic tiles, which can have very sharp edges. Try it out as a helper, [and] you will know right away if this is a job for you. On the other hand, if you are a creative person, this might be a great job for you. Tile setting is very creative. That's the best thing about this job. It's always different. Even if you are working with the same tile, you are always doing a different configuration. The only time it gets boring is when you are working in a large building, like a nursing home, for example. You may have one tile for all the floors or all the bathrooms throughout the entire building. The good thing is that after the first few, you won't have to think about what you are going to do, but on the other hand, it can get monotonous.

I didn't do an apprenticeship or have any formal training. There is no license to be a tile setter like there is to be a plumber or an electrician, because we all do our job differently. Plumbers and electricians have to follow a certain standard way of doing things. Tile setters do not. We all have our own personal style. There are unions, though, but I don't belong to one anymore.

As a tile setter I would say that my primary responsibility is to make sure I do a good job and that everyone is satisfied with my work. That's my ultimate goal. Of equal importance is to first speak with the proper representative for the job, which would be the homeowner or the general contractor—whoever is paying me—to find out exactly what I will be doing. I need to figure out how much time it will take, what materials I will need and how much. I will need to do the right underlaying, that's the surface I put down before I set the tiles. I need to know what pattern I will be doing, whether it's a square set or a diagonal—there are a multitude of patterns I could be doing. Then I have to schedule the job and do the work. So, depending on the application, there are different types of tiles that need different types of setting. There are ceramic, marble, granite, quarry, porcelain, and limestone tiles. Depending on which of these you are setting, you will need either mortar [a mixture of cement or lime with sand and water], mastic [a type of sticky pastelike cement], or thinset [a special type of mortar] with which to set your tiles. The tiles come in all different sizes. The smallest is a 1-inch-by-1-inch [2.5 centimeters by 2.5 centimeters] tile. The largest I have ever set is an 18-inch-by-18-inch [46 cm by 46 cm] tile. That's the largest tile I have the tools and equipment for. But there are even larger tiles. There are different tools used to accommodate the tiles the bigger they get.

This work is very dependent on the economy. More houses go up when the economy is good, so there is more work for the tile setters. The weather plays a key role in our employment as well, but in a domino effect sort of way. I work indoors, and so the weather doesn't make much difference to me one way or another. However, it makes a great deal of difference to the plumbers and electricians, and I can't work on a new building until they have already been there and done their work. A tile setter needs heat (in the winter), water, and electricity to do his work.

In fact, this is one of the great things about being a tile setter. I am one of the last people to enter the project. By the time I get to the house, the plumbing, electricity, and everything have been done, [and] the walls and floors are in place. The only thing[s] left to do [are] the tiling . . . the painting, and [the] carpet laying. So it's pretty quiet by the time those guys and I get there.

Back to our pay, though. Starting as a helper, depending on whom you work for, you may just make minimum wage or a little more. The guy who is working for me right now, I started him at $10 an hour. It's hard to say exactly how much a tile setter will get paid because we are paid by the foot. But you can estimate that an accomplished tile setter will make about $30 an hour. Today, I had a 150-square-foot [14 sq m] floor to tile. I had to put in an underlay first, so that has to be factored into my time as well. I worked from 7:00 this morning to about 12:30 today. When the tile setter is paid, he makes more money if he is doing more than just a standard pattern. So, I made about $2.50 per square foot today. I make about $60,000 a year. This is above average. A self-employed tile setter will make roughly $35,000 to

$60,000 a year. If you have guys working for you, they will bring in more money for you. The guys will make about $20 to $30 an hour before taxes and insurance. There are bids for jobs, so obviously the pay varies depending on who you are and what you do, how you do it, and so forth.

Getting the job is all about how good you are. Referrals are a huge help. If your referrals are good, they don't question your prices.

I do bathrooms, kitchens, laundry rooms, dining rooms, basement floors, [and] mudrooms. Mostly I work in homes, but I sometimes work in institutions such as schools, hospitals, and nursing homes as well. When you work residential, it's either newly constructed homes or remodeling. When you work commercial, you are doing brand-new larger buildings, such as banks, hospitals, and apartment buildings from the ground up. You'll make more money if you work residential.

Since I work for myself, I like being the last guy to come in and give an estimate for a job. I can tell the homeowner, "I can beat that price," on whatever the lowest price is that he's been quoted. I can do the work for less if I really need the work. It's nice, however, when you have someone else doing the estimate and bidding for you, you know, if someone else is in charge.

Study mathematics in school if you want to become a tile setter. There's a lot of math in this job. You have to figure out the best layout, the best fit for the area you have to work in. I recommend you read a magazine called the TileLetter, *which is free to members of the NTCA.*

AND JUST A NOTE ABOUT ROOF TILING

Another type of tiling that might interest you, especially if you enjoy working outdoors, is roof tiling. You will need to complete a roof tiling apprenticeship before you can begin a career in roof tiling. The best way to go about finding an apprenticeship is to look for an employer who is willing to supervise your learning and your work. Before you set out on this journey, however, you will want to complete your high school education. You will learn your trade both on-the-job and off (by doing some learning, reading, and practicing on your own).

Once you have finished your apprenticeship and are ready to get to work, you will have to decide whether you want to work for someone or for yourself. Many roof tilers find work with small companies that fix roofs or actually supply the necessary roofs to structures. You may also work for a tile manufacturing company.

AFTERWORD

If you were uncertain about your future career path before you began to read this book, now that you have read through the pages, you should have a good idea about what you might like to spend your work years doing. You have read about one or more of five trades—electrician, plumber, mason, carpenter, and tiler. You now know what each of these jobs entails. You have learned about what a workday might be like, what weather conditions you might find yourself working in, what type of climate best supports the work, whether you will work indoors or out-doors or both, and about the seasons that will support the most work opportunities. You know about the pay scale for the trades, from a starting salary to the highest amount of money that you might be able to make. You have read about the possibilities of working for yourself or for small or large companies. You have a good idea about what an apprenticeship for each trade requires and what you can expect to study in school. And perhaps most important, you have read firsthand the words of craftspeople who have found gainful employment and exciting careers in each of the trades.

The rest is up to you. If you decide that you have the interest and the talent to pursue one of these exciting and creative careers, follow the hints and suggestions in the chapter that addresses the trade of your choice. Visit your local library or your favorite bookstore to review, check out, or purchase the books that are listed in the For Further Reading section of this book. Go online and check out some of the Web sites mentioned in this book. Find out as much as you can about your career interest so that you are sure to get the training and education you will need to pursue your dreams for success.

You have chosen a bright and lucrative path and the future is yours, for as mason Terry Mulligan says, "If you have a trade, any trade, you should never be out of work."

GLOSSARY

Allen wrench A six-sided hand tool that is used to hold or twist a nut or bolt.

apprentice Someone who learns a trade or art by gaining experience while working under the supervision of a skilled worker.

apprenticeship A method by which a person works for an employer as an apprentice in a chosen trade and learns the necessary skills, knowledge, and attitudes to become a qualified craftsperson.

aptitude Natural ability.

blueprint A detailed plan of something to be done.

brattices Boards used for support.

Bureau of Labor Statistics (BLS) An agency of the U.S. Department of Labor that is the principal fact-finding office for the U.S. government in the broad field of labor economics and statistics. The BLS features statistical data on employment and unemployment, employment projections, prices, living conditions, productivity and technology, working conditions, and international economies.

cabinetry The building of cabinets and furniture in general.

carpenter A worker who builds or repairs things made of wood.

carpentry The building of structures.

cinder block A hollow rectangular building block made of cement and coal cinders.

conduit A tube that houses electrical wiring.

contractor A person who acquires the jobs for his or her workers.

cupola In architecture, a small dome or similar structure on a roof; a rounded roof or ceiling.

dexterity Skill and ease in bodily activity.

electrician A person who installs or repairs electrical equipment.

finish carpentry The paneling, trim, doors, and other details of a building.

GED (general equivalency diploma) A written exam diploma rather than an actual high school diploma.

HVAC Heating, ventilation, and air conditioning.

inside wireman An electrical worker who installs the power, lighting, various controls, and other electrical equipment in commercial and industrial buildings.

internship Time spent getting practical experience on the job.

joist Any of the parallel horizontal beams set from wall to wall in a structure to support the boards of a floor or ceiling.

journeyman A worker who has learned a trade and usually works for another person by the day.

kiln A furnace or oven that may be heated for the purpose of hardening, burning, or drying a material such as earthenware, pottery, porcelain, or lumber.

laborer A person who labors, especially a wage-earning worker, skilled or unskilled, whose work is characterized largely by physical exertion.

lineman One who sets up and prepares for the job to be done.

master An artist of great skill.

mortar A mixture of sand and lime or cement and lime with sand and water used between bricks or stones in building, or as plaster.

OSHA Occupational Safety and Health Administration. An agency in the U.S. Department of Labor whose mission is to help maintain a safe and healthy work environment for America's workers.

outside lineman An electrical worker who installs distribution and transmission lines that move power from the power plant to homes, businesses, and factories.

pipe fitter A plumber.

residential wireman An electrical worker who specializes in the installation of all the electrical systems in homes.

rough carpentry The framing or building of walls and roofs of a new structure.

structural carpenter Carpenter who builds the framework of a structure.

terrazzo A mosaic flooring consisting of small pieces of marble or granite set in mortar and given a high polish.

vocational school Schooling that is work-related or in which one learns a trade.

plumb bob A pear-shaped or globular weight, ending in a point, suspended from the end of a plumb line.

plumbing A plumber's occupation or trade; the apparatus (as pipes and fixtures) concerned in the distribution and use of water in a building.

plumb line A line directed to the Earth's center of gravity; a cord suspending a lead weight, or plumb, used in determining vertical direction.

raceway A channel for loosely holding electrical wires in buildings.

roto stripper An attachment with steel wires and that is used on an electric drill for removing paint, varnish, and rust on wood, plastic, fiberglass, masonry, and metal.

service conductor The supply conductor that extends from the street main or transformer to the service equipment of the structure being supplied.

service drop The run of cables from the power company's aerial power lines to the point of connection to a customer's premises.

stucco Plaster or cement of any kind used as a coating for surfacing inside or outside walls, moldings, etc.

studs The smaller upright boards in the framing of the walls of a building to which sheathing, paneling, or other materials are fastened.

transformer A static electrical device that, by electromagnetic induction, regenerates AC power from one circuit to another. A transformer is also used to change voltage from one level to another.

trowel To spread, smooth, shape, or dig with a trowel, which is a small hand tool with a flat metal blade.

FOR MORE INFORMATION

PLUG INTO THE NETWORK

For a comprehensive look at all the trade and vocational schools that offer courses in your trade of choice, see *Vocational and Technical Schools: East and West* (Lawrenceville, NJ: Peterson's, 2003).

Listed below are some of the colleges that offer courses in the building and construction trades.

CARPENTER

Alabama
Bishop State Community College (Mobile)
Gadsden State Community College (Gadsden)
John M. Patterson State Technical College (Montgomery)
Lawson State Community College (Birmingham)
Northwest-Shoals Community College (Muscle Shoals)
Reid State Technical College (Evergreen)

Arizona
Gateway Community College (Phoenix)
North American Technical College (Phoenix)
Northland Pioneer College (Holbrook)

Arkansas
Crowley's Ridge Technical Institute (Forrest City)
Quapaw Technical Institute (Hot Springs)

California
Laney College (Oakland)
North Valley Occupational Center Pacoima Skills Center (Mission Hills)

Colorado
T. H. Pickens Technical Center (Aurora)

Florida
Charlotte Vocational-Technical Center (Port Charlotte)
David G. Erwin Technical Center (Tampa)
Florida Community College at Jacksonville (Jacksonville)
Indian River Community College (Fort Pierce)

Lee County Vocational
High Tech Center Central
(Fort Myers)
Manatee Technical Institute
(Bradenton)
North Florida Community
College (Madison)
Okaloosa Applied Technology
Center (Ft. Walton Beach)
Pinellas Technical
Education Center–St.
Petersburg (St. Petersburg)
Radford M. Locklin Technical
Center (Milton)
Sarasota County Technical
Institute (Sarasota)
Seminole Community
College (Sanford)
Suwannee-Hamilton Area
Vocational Technical and Adult
Education Center (Live Oak)
Taylor Technical Institute (Perry)
Tom P. Haney Technical Center
(Panama City)
West Technical Education Center
(Belle Glade)
Withlacoochee Technical
Institute (Inverness)

Georgia
Albany Technical
Institute (Albany)
Columbus Technical College
(Columbus)
Griffin Technical College (Griffin)
Gwinnett Technical College
(Lawrenceville)
Lanier Technical Institute
(Oakland)
Turner Jobs Corps
Center (Albany)

Hawaii
Hawaii Community College (Hilo)

Honolulu Community College
(Honolulu)
Kauai Community
College (Lihue)

Idaho
North Idaho College (Coeur
d'Alene)

Indiana
Charles A. Prosser School of
Technology (New Albany)

Iowa
Indian Hills Community
College–Centerville
Campus (Centerville)
Iowa Central Community College
(Fort Dodge)
Iowa Lakes Community College
(Estherville)
Northeast Iowa Community
College (Calmar)
North Iowa Area Community
College (Mason City)
Northwest Iowa Community
College (Sheldon)
Southwestern Community
College (Creston)
Western Iowa Tech Community
College (Sioux City)

Kansas
Flint Hills Technical College
(Emporia)
Hutchinson Community College
and Area Vocational School
(Hutchinson)
Manhattan Area Technical
College (Manhattan)
North Central Kansas Technical
College (Beloit)
Southwest Kansas Technical
School (Liberal)

Wichita Area Technical College
(Wichita)

Kentucky
Christian County Vocational
School (Hopkinsville)
Clay County Area Technical
Center (Manchester)
Cumberland Valley Technical
College–Harlan (Harlan)
Harrodsburg Area Technology
Center (Harrodsburg)
Jefferson Technical College
(Louisville)
Kentucky Tech–Clark County Area
Technology Center (Winchester)
Kentucky Tech–Elizabethtown
Campus (Elizabethtown)
Kentucky Tech–Hazard State
Vocational Tech School (Hazard)
Knott County Area Technology
Center (Hindman)
Lee County Area Technology
Center (Beattyville)
Madisonville Technical College
(Madisonville)
Mayo Regional Technical Center
(Paintsville)
Meade County Area Tecnical
Center (Brandenburg)
Northern Kentucky Technical
College (Covington)
Owensboro Technical College
(Owensboro)
Rowan Technical College
(Morehead)
West Kentucky Tech (Paducah)

Massachusetts
Assabet Valley Regional
Vocational Technical School
(Marlborough)
North Bennet Street School
(Boston)

Michigan
Mott Community College (Flint)
Northern Michigan University
(Marquette)

Mississippi
Hinds Community College
(Raymond)
Meridian Community College
(Meridian)
Mississippi Gulf Coast
Community College
(Perkinston)
Southwest Mississippi
Community College (Summit)

New Jersey
Cape May County Technical
School District (Cape May
Courthouse)
Technical Institute of Camden
County (Sicklerville)

New York
Oswego County BOCES (Mexico)
Putnam Westchester BOCES
(Yorktown Heights)
State University of New York
College of Agriculture and
Technology at Morrisville
(Morrisville)

North Carolina
Asheville-Buncombe
Technical Community
College (Asheville)
Bladen Community College
(Dublin)
Cleveland Community College
(Shelby)
Pitt Community College
(Greenville)
South Piedmont Community
College (Polkton)

Vance-Granville Community
College (Henderson)

Pennsylvania
Jefferson County–Dubois Area
Vocational Technology–
Practical Nursing
(Reynoldsville)
Orleans Technical Institute
(Philadelphia)
Pennsylvania College of
Technology (Williamsport)
Triangle Tech, Inc. (Pittsburg)

South Carolina
Bob Jones University
(Greenville)
Midlands Technical College
(Columbia)

Virginia
J. Sargeant Reynolds Community
College (Richmond)

Wisconsin
Chippewa Valley Technical
College (Eau Claire)

ELECTRICIAN

Alabama
Bishop State Community College
(Mobile)
Douglas MacArthur State
Technical College (Opp)
Gadsden State Community
College (Gadsden)
George Corley Wallace State
Community College (Selma)
Lawson State Community
College (Birmingham)
Northwest-Shoals Community
College (Muscle Shoals)

Shelton State Community
College (Tuscaloosa)

Arizona
North American Technical
College (Phoenix)
Northland Pioneer College
(Holbrook)

California
Educorp Career College (Long
Beach)
Harbor Occupational Center
(San Pedro)
Orange Coast College
(Costa Mesa)

Colorado
T. H. Pickens Technical Center
(Aurora)

Connecticut
Industrial Management Training
Institute (Waterbury)
New England Technical
Institute of Connecticut, Inc.
(New Britain)

Florida
Atlantic Vocational-Technical
Center (Coconut Creek)
Central Florida Community
College (Ocala)
Charlotte Vocational-Technical
Center (Port Charlotte)
Florida Community College of
Jacksonville (Jacksonville)
Indian River Community College
(Fort Pierce)
Lee County Vocational High Tech
Center Central (Fort Myers)
Manatee Technical Institute
(Bradenton)
Mid-Florida Tech (Orlando)

Radford M. Locklin Technical
Center (Milton)
Ridge Technical Center (Winter
Haven)
Sarasota County Technical
Institute (Sarasota)
South Technical Education
Center (Boynton Beach)
Withlacoochee Technical
Institute (Inverness)

Georgia
Albany Technical Institute
(Albany)
Augusta Technical College
(Augusta)
Griffin Technical College (Griffin)
Heart of Georgia Technical
Institute (Dublin)
North Georgia Technical College
(Clarksville)
West Central Technical College
(Carrollton)

Hawaii
Honolulu Community College
(Honolulu)
Kauai Community College (Lihue)

Idaho
Idaho State University (Pocatello)

Illinois
Coyne American Institute
Incorporated (Chicago)
Illinois Valley Community
College (Oglesby)
John Wood Community College
(Quincy)
Triton College (River Grove)

Iowa
Northeast Iowa Community
College (Calmar)

Western Iowa Tech Community
College (Sioux City)

Kansas
North Central Kansas Area
Vocational–Technical
School–Hays Campus (Hays)
North Central Kansas Technical
College (Beloit)
Northwest Kansas Area
Vocational Technical School
(Goodland)
Southeast Kansas Area Vocational
Technical School (Coffeyville)

Kentucky
Belfry Area Technology Center
(Belfry)
Christian County Vocational
School (Hopkinsville)
Cumberland Valley Technical
College–Harlan (Harlan)
Cumberland Valley Technical
College–Middlesboro
(Middlesboro)
Harrodsburg Area Technology
Center (Harrodsburg)
Kentucky Tech–Elizabethtown
Campus (Elizabethtown)
Kentucky Tech–Hazard State
Vocational Tech School (Hazard)
Kentucky Tech–Mayfield-Graves
County Area Technology
Center (Mayfield)
Knott County Area Technology
Center (Hindman)
Lee County Area Technology
Center (Beattyville)
Madisonville Technical College
(Madisonville)
Mayo Regional Technology
Center (Paintsville)
Meade County Area Technology
Center (Brandenburg)

Northern Kentucky Technical
College (Covington)
Owensboro Technical College
(Owensboro)
Rowan Technical College
(Morehead)
West Kentucky Tech (Paducah)

Louisiana

Delgado Community College
(New Orleans)
Elaine P. Nunez Community
College (Chalmette)
Louisiana Technical College–
Delta-Ouachita Campus (West
Monroe)
Louisiana Technical College–
Jefferson Campus (Metairie)
Louisiana Technical College–
Lafourche Campus (Thibodaux)
Louisiana Technical College
(Morgan City)
Louisiana Technical
College–Natchitoches Campus
(Natchitoches)
Louisiana Technical College–
Shreveport–Bossier Campus
(Shreveport)
Louisiana Technical
College–Slidell Campus (Slidell)
Louisiana Technical College–
Sowela Campus (Lake Charles)
Louisiana Technical
College–Teche Area Campus
(New Iberia)
Sullivan Technical Institute
(Bogalusa)

Maine

Eastern Maine Technical College
(Bangor)

Maryland

Anne Arundel Community
College (Arnold)

Massachusetts

Assabet Valley Regional
Vocational-Technical School
(Marlborough)
Benjamin Franklin Institute of
Technology (Boston)
Peterson School of Steam
Engineering (Woburn)

Minnesota

Alexandria Technical College
(Alexandria)
Hennepin Technical College
(Brooklyn Park)
Lake Superior College (Duluth)
Minneapolis Community and
Technical College (Minneapolis)
Minnesota State College–
Southeast Technical–Red Wing
(Red Wing)
Northwest Technical College
(East Grand Forks)
Northwest Technical College
(Wadena)
Rochester Community and
Technical College (Rochester)
St. Cloud Technical College (St.
Cloud)
St. Paul Technical College (St. Paul)

Mississippi

Hinds Community College
(Raymond)
Meridian Community College
(Meridian)
Mississippi Gulf Coast
Community College
(Perkinston)
Southwest Mississippi
Community College (Summit)

Missouri

Davis H. Hart Mexico Area
Vocational-Technical School
(Mexico)

Lebanon Technology and Career Center (Lebanon)

Northwest Technical School (Maryville)

Ozark Mountain Technical Center (Mountain Grove)

Perryville Area Career and Technology Center (Perryville)

Pike/Lincoln Tech Center (Eolia)

Vatterott College (Kansas City)

Vatterott College (Springfield)

Montana
Miles Community College (Miles Center)

Nebraska
Central Community College–Grand Island Campus (Grand Island)

New Jersey
Technical Institute of Camden County (Sicklerville)

New Mexico
Albuquerque Technical Vocational Institute (Albuquerque)

Crownpoint Institute of Technology (Crownpoint)

New York
Adult Practical Nursing–Albany BOCES (Albany)

Berk Trade and Business School (New York City)

Lewis A. Wilson Technological Center (Dix Hills)

Oswego County BOCES (Mexico)

Putnam-Westchester BOCES (Yorktown Heights)

North Carolina
Carteret Community College (Morehead City)

Cleveland Community College (Shelby)

Coastal Carolina Community College (Jacksonville)

Fayetteville Technical Community College (Fayetteville)

Haywood Community College (Clyde)

Nash Community College (Rock Mount)

Southwestern Community College (Whiteville)

Surry Community College (Dobson)

Tri-County Community College (Murphy)

Wake Technical Community College (Raleigh)

Ohio
Ashtabula County Joint Vocational School (Jefferson)

O. C. Collins Career Center (Chesapeake)

Scioto County Joint Vocational School District (Lucasville)

Oklahoma
Autry Technology Center (Enid)

Metro Area Vocational Technical School District 22 (Oklahoma City)

Pennsylvania
CHI Institute, RETS Campus (Broomall)

CHI Institute (Southhampton)

Fayette Institute of Commerce and Technology, Inc. (Uniontown)

Greater Altoona Career and Technology Center (Altoona)

Greater Johnstown Career and
Technology Center (Johnstown)
Harrisburg Area Community
College (Harrisburg)
Luzerne County Community
College (Nanticoke)
Orleans Technical Institute
(Philadelphia)
Pennsylvania College of
Technology (Williamsport)
Triangle Tech, Inc.–Erie
School (Erie)
Triangle Tech, Inc.–Greensburg
Center (Greensburg)
Triangle Tech, Inc. (Pittsburg)

South Carolina
Midlands Technical College
(Columbia)

South Dakota
Mitchell Technical Institute
(Mitchell)

Tennessee
Northeast State Technical
Community College (Blountville)
Tennessee Technology Center at
Athens (Athens)
Tennessee Technology Center at
Knoxville (Knoxville)

Texas
Texarkana College (Texarkana)

Utah
Utah Basin Applied Technology
Center (Roosevelt)

Virginia
Southside Training Skill Center
(Crewe)
Thomas Nelson Community
College (Hampton)

Washington
Bates Technical College
(Tacoma)
Lake Washington Technical
College (Kirkland)
Lower Columbus College
(Longview)
Spokane Community College
(Spokane)

West Virginia
Academy of Careers and
Technology (Beckley)
Carver Career Center (Charleston)
James Rumsey Technical
Institute (Martinsburg)
Monongalia County Technical
Education Center
(Morgantown)

PLUMBER

Alabama
Bishop State Community College
(Mobile)
Lawson State Community
College (Birmingham)

Alaska
Testing Institute of Alaska, Inc.
(Anchorage)

Arizona
North American Technical
College (Phoenix)

California
Educorp Career College (Long
Beach)

Connecticut
Industrial Management Training
Institute (Waterbury)

Florida

Atlantic Vocational-Technical
Center (Coconut Creek)
Florida Community College at
Jacksonville (Jacksonville)
Hillsboro Community College
(Tampa)
Indian River Community College
(Fort Pierce)
Lee County Vocational High
Tech Center Central (Fort
Meyers)
Mid-Florida Tech (Orlando)
Pinellas Technical Education
Center–St. Petersburg (St.
Petersburg)
Radford M. Locklin Technical
Center (Milton)
Seminole Community College
(Sanford)

Georgia

Griffin Technical
College (Griffin)

Iowa

Northeast Iowa Community
College (Calmer)
Western Iowa Community
College (Sioux City)

Kentucky

Jefferson Technical College
(Louisville)
Kentucky Tech–Elizabethtown
Campus (Elizabethtown)

Maine

Northern Maine Technical
College (Presque Isle)

Massachusetts

Cape Cod Plumbing School, Inc.
(Hyannis)

George W. Gould Institute
(Burlington)
Peterson School of Steam
Engineering (Woburn)

Michigan

Henry Ford Community College
(Dearborn)
Mott Community College (Flint)

Minnesota

Northwest Technical College
(East Grand Forks)
Northwest Technical College
(Wadena)
St. Cloud Technical College
(St. Cloud)
St. Paul Technical College (St. Paul)

Mississippi

Mississippi Gulf Coast Community
College (Perkinston)

New Jersey

Hudson County Schools of
Technology (North Bergen)
Technical Institute of Camden
County (Sicklerville)

New Mexico

Albuquerque Technical Vocational
Institute (Albuquerque)

New York

Berk Trade and Business School
(New York City)
Lewis A. Wilson Technological
Center (Dix Hills)
Putnam-Westchester BOCES
(Yorktown Heights)

North Carolina

Cleveland Community College
(Shelby)

Fayetteville Technical Community
College (Fayetteville)
Southeastern Community
College (Whiteville)
Southwestern Community
College (Sylva)
Tri-County Community College
(Murphy)
Wake Technical Community
College (Raleigh)

Oklahoma
Great Plains Area Vocational-
Technical School (Lawton)
Kiamichi Area Vocational Tech
School–Atoka (Atoka)
Kiamichi Area Vocational Tech
School, School District
7–Stigler (Stigler)
Kiamichi Area Vocational Tech
School, School District
7–Talihina (Talihina)
Meridian Technology Center
(Stillwater)
Metro Area Vocational
Technical School District 22
(Oklahoma City)
Northwest Technology
Center (Alva)
Pontotoc Technology
Center (Ada)

Oregon
Portland Community College
(Portland)

Pennsylvania
Lebanon County Area
Vocational Technical School
(Lebanon)
Luzerne County Community
College (Nanticoke)
Orleans Technical Institute
(Philadelphia)

Pennsylvania College of
Technology (Williamsport)

South Dakota
Western Dakota Technical
Institute (Rapid City)

Utah
Utah Basin Applied Technology
Center (Roosevelt)

Virginia
Central Virginia Community
College (Lynchburg)

Washington
Bates Technical College
(Tacoma)
Columbia Basin College (Pasco)
Renton Technical College
(Renton)
Spokane Community College
(Spokane)

Wisconsin
Chippewa Valley Technical
College (Eau Claire)

Wyoming
Laramie County Community
College (Cheyenne)

MASON AND TILE SETTER

Alabama
Bishop State Community College
(Mobile)
Gadsden State Community
College (Gadsden)
George Corley Wallace
Community College (Selma)
Reid State Technical College
(Evergreen)

Wallace Community College–
Sparks Campus (Eufaula)

Florida
Lee County Vocational
High Tech Center Central
(Fort Meyers)
Miami Skill Center (Miami)
Radford M. Locklin Technical
Center (Milton)
Suwanee-Hamilton Area
Vocational, Technical, and Adult
Education Center (Live Oak)

Georgia
Turner Jobs Corps Center (Albany)

Kansas
Southwest Kansas Technical
School

Kentucky
Christian County Vocational
School (Hopkinsville)
Northern Kentucky Technical
College (Covington)

Michigan
Mott Community College (Flint)

Mississippi
Hinds Community College
(Raymond)

Missouri
Rolla Technical Institute (Rolla)

New Jersey
Technical Institute of Camden
College (Sicklerville)

New York
Oswego County BOCES (Mexico)

North Carolina
Fayetteville Technical Community
College (Fayetteville)
Pitt Community College
(Greenville)
South Piedmont Community
College (Polkton)
Southwestern Community
College (Whiteville)
Tri-County Community College
(Murphy)

Ohio
Fairfield Career Center (Carroll)

Oklahoma
Great Plains Area Vocational-
Technical School (Lawton)
Meridian Technology Center
(Stillwater)

Pennsylvania
Greater Johnstown Career and
Technology Center (Johnstown)

Tennessee
Tennessee Technology Center at
Crossville (Crossville)
Tennessee Technology Center at
Morristown (Morristown)

Virginia
Norfolk Skills Center (Norfolk)

West Virginia
James Rumsey Technical
Institute (Martinsburg)

RESOURCES

There is a seemingly inexhaustible supply of resources for all of these trades. While a book of this size cannot possibly list every single resource available, the following is a good sampling of the information that is accessible.

CARPENTER RESOURCES

Associated General Contractors of America
333 John Carlyle Street, Suite 200
Alexandria, VA 22314
(703) 548-3118
Web site: http://www.agc.org

Habitat for Humanity International
121 Habitat Street
Americus, GA 31709
(229) 924-6935, ext. 2551
Web site: http://www.habitat.org

Home Builders Institute
1201 15th Street NW
6th Floor
Washington, DC 20005
(202) 371-0600
Web site: http://www.hbi.org

United Brotherhood of Carpenters and
  Joiners of America
101 Constitution Avenue NW
Washington, DC 20001
(202) 546-6206
Web site: http://www.carpenters.org

PLUMBER RESOURCES

Additional information on the occupation of plumber is available from the Bureau of Labor Statistics' *Occupational Outlook Handbook* (Chicago, IL: VGM Careerbooks, 2004).

National Association of Plumbing-Heating-Cooling
  Contractors (NAPHCC)
180 South Washington Street
P.O. Box 6808
Falls Church, VA 22040
(800) 535-7694
Web site: http://www.phccweb.org

United Association of Journeymen and Apprentices of
  the Plumbing and Pipefitting Industry of the United
  States and Canada
901 Massachusetts Avenue NW
Washington, DC 20001
(202) 628-5823
Web site: http://www.ua.org

*Nonunion training and apprenticeship programs
are administered by local chapters of the following
organizations:*

Associated Builders and Contractors
1300 North Seventeenth Street, Suite 800
Rosslyn, VA 22209
(703) 812-2000

Home Builders Institute (HBI)
National Association of Home Builders (NAHB)
1201 15th Street NW
Washington, DC 20005
(202) 371-0600
Web site: http://www.hbi.org

U.S. Department of Labor
Frances Perkins Building
200 Constitution Avenue NW
Washington, DC 20210
(866) 4-USA-DOL (487-2365)
Web site: http://www.dol.gov/dol/findit.htm

ELECTRICIAN RESOURCES

Associated Builders and Contractors (ABC)
4250 North Fairfax Drive, 9th Floor
Arlington, VA 22203
(703) 812-2000
Web site: http://www.abc.org

Home Builders Institute (HBI)
National Association of Home Builders (NAHB)
1201 15th Street NW
Washington, DC 20005
(202) 371-0600
Web site: http://www.hbi.org

Independent Electrical Contractors, Inc.
2010A Eisenhower Avenue
Alexandria, VA 22314
(703) 549-7351
Web site: http://www.ieci.org

International Brotherhood of Electrical
  Workers (IBEW)
1125 15th Street NW
Washington, DC 20005
(202) 833-7000
Web site: http://www.ibew.org

International Society of Certified
  Electronics Technicians
3608 Pershing Avenue
Fort Worth, TX 76107-4527
(817) 921-9101
Web site: http://www.iscet.org

National Electrical Contractors
  Association (NECA)
3 Metro Center, Suite 1100
Bethesda, MD 20814
(301) 657-3110
Web site: http://www.necanet.org

National Joint Apprenticeship and
  Training Committee (NJATC)
301 Prince George's Boulevard, Suite D
Upper Marlboro, MD 20774
Web site: http://www.njatc.org

MASON RESOURCES

American Ceramic Society
P.O. Box 6136
Westerville, OH 43086-6136
(614) 890-4700
e-mail: info@ceramics.org
Web site: http://www.acers.org

American Concrete Institute
P.O. Box 9094
Farmington Hills, MI 48333
Web site: http://www.aci-int.org

American Concrete Pumping Association
606 Enterprise Drive
Lewis Center, OH 43035
(614) 431-5618
Web site: http://www.concretepumpers.com

BAC (International Union of Bricklayers and
  Allied Craftworkers)
1776 Eye Street NW
Washington, DC 20006
(202) 783-3788
Web site: http://bacweb.org

Brick Industry Association
1490 Commerce Park Drive
Reston, VA 20191-1525
(703) 620-0100
e-mail: brickinfo@bia.org
Web site: http://www.brickinfo.org

Ceramic Glazed Masonry Institution
P.O. Box 35575
Canton, OH 44735
(330) 649-9551
e-mail: cgmi@neo.rr.com
Web site: http://www.cgmi.org

International Masonry Institute Head Office
The James Brice House
42 East Street
Annapolis, MD 21401
(410) 280-1305
Web site: http://www.imiweb.org

Mason Contractors Association of America
33 South Roselle Road

Schaumburg, IL 60193
(847) 301-0001; (800) 536-2225
Web site: http://www.masoncontractors.org

Masonry Advisory Council
1480 Renaissance Drive, Suite 302
Park Ridge, IL 60068
(847) 297-6704
Web site: http://www.maconline.org

Masonry Institute of America
386 Beech Avenue, Suite 4
Torrance, CA 90501
(310) 328-4400
Web site: http://www.masonryinstitute.org

Masonry Magazine
33 South Roselle Road
Schaumburg, IL 60193
(800) 536-2225
Web site: http://www.masonrymagazine.com/
  links.html

The Masonry Society
3970 Broadway, Suite 201-D
Boulder, CO 80304-1135
(303) 939-9700
Web site: http://www.masonrysociety.org

National Concrete Masonry Association
13750 Sunrise Valley Drive
Herndon, VA 20171-4662
(703) 713-1900
e-mail: ncma@ncma.org
Web site: http://www.ncma.org

TILER RESOURCES

National Tile Contractors Association (NTCA)
P.O. Box 13629
Jackson, MS 39236
(601) 939-2071
Web site: http://www.tile-assn.com
The *TileLetter* is a free monthly magazine published by the NTCA and written specifically for the tiling industry. More than 20,000 firms receive *TileLetter* each month, and at least 50,000 tilers read the magazine. You can get more information by visiting the NTCA's Web site at http://www.tile-assn.com/tileletter to join the NTCA.

To receive the NTCA Reference Manual, the "industry's finest installation handbook," free of charge, become an NTCA member, and to obtain information about NTCA workshops, to find installation videos, available in both DVD and VHS, and training manuals (available individually or as a complete set), and to learn more about the NTCA's three-year in-house training curriculum apprenticeship program, visit: http://www.tile-assn.com/membership/why_join.

National Terrazzo and Mosaic Association
201 N. Maple, Suite 208
Purcellville, VA 20132
(800) 323-9736
Web site: http://www.ntma.com

The Tile Contractors Association of America
4 East 113th Terrace
Kansas City, MO 64114
Web site: http://www.tcaainc.org

Tile, Marble, Terrazzo, Finishers, Shopworkers, and
  Granite Cutters International Union
101 Constitution Avenue NW
Washington, DC 20001

United Brotherhood of Carpenters and Joiners of America
101 Constitution Avenue NW
Washington, DC 20001
(202) 546-6206
Web site: http://www.carpenters.org

OTHER HELPFUL RESOURCES

American Contracting Exchange
603 Millwood Drive
Fallston, MD 21047
(800) 892-0007
Web site: http://www.homerepair.org

Associated Construction Distributors International
1605 SE Delaware Avenue, Suite B
Ankeny, IA 50021
(515) 964-1335
Web site: http://www.acdi.net

Association of General Contractors of America
333 John Carlyle Street, Suite 200
Alexandria, VA 22314
(703) 548-3118
Web site: http://www.agc.org

Chicago Women in Trades
1657 West Adams, Suite 401
Chicago, IL 60612
(312) 942-1444
Web site: http://www.chicagowomenintrades.org

Construction Safety Council
4100 Madison Street
Hillside, IL 60162
(708) 544-2082
Web site: http://www.buildsafe.org

National Association of Women in Construction
327 South Adams Street
Fort Worth, TX 76104
(817) 877-5551
Web site: http://www.nawic.org

Professional Career Development Institute (PCDI)
430 Technology Parkway
Norcross, GA 30092
(800) 223-4542
Web site: http://www.pcdi.edu

Women Construction Owners and Executives USA
4410A Connecticut Avenue NW
Washington, DC 20008
(800) 788-3548
Web site: http://www.wcoeusa.org

CAREER-RELATED WEB SITES IN THE BUILDING AND CONSTRUCTION TRADES

American Society of Sanitary Engineering (ASSE) (http://www.asse-plumbing.org)
Building and Construction ITO (http://www.bcito.org.nz/apprentice/tiling.htm)
Career Zone (http://www.nycareerzone.org)
Construction Bookstore (http://www.bookmarki.com)
Contractor's License Reference Site (http://www.contractors-license.org)

Division of Professional Licensure (http://www.mass.gov/dpl/home.htm)

The Electrical Contractor Network: Electrical and Construction Bookstore (http://www.electrical-contractor.net/The_Store/Electrical.htm)

Electrician.com (http://www.electrician.com)

Electrician's Toolbox, Etc. (http://www.elec-toolbox.com)

Findaplumber.com (http://www.findaplumber.com)

FlipDog.com (http://flipdog.monster.com)

IEEE, the Institute of Electrical and Electronics Engineers, Inc. (http://www.ieee.org)

Ihireconstruction.com (http://www.ihireconstruction.com)

Iseek.org (http://www.iseek.org)

JobGuide 2003 (http://jobguide.thegoodguides.com.au/statespecific.cfm?jobid = 726&state_id = NT)

Licensed Occupations (http://www.acinet.org/acinet/lois_start.asp)

Masonry-training.com (http://www.masonry-training.com)

Occupational Outlook Handbook, 2004-2005 edition, (http://www.bls.gov/oco/home.htm)

Professional Career Development Institute (http://career-colleges.org)

Skoool.ie Interactive Learning (http://www.skoool.ie/skoool/careermatters.asp?id = 1825)

SUNY Delhi, College of Technology (http://techdivision.delhi.edu/Carpentry, % 20Woodworking, % 20Masonry/CARPcareers.htm)

TCIDS—Tennessee Information Career Delivery System (http://www.tcids.utk.edu)

UA—United Association of Plumbers and Pipefitters (http://www.state.ma.us/reg/boards/pl)

United Association of Journeymen and Apprentices of the Plumbing, Pipefitting, Sprinkler Fitting Industry of the United States and Canada (http://12.4.18.10/index.htm)

The United Brotherhood of Carpenters and Joiners of America (http://www.carpenters.org)

U.S. Department of Labor Employment and Training Administration (http://www.doleta.org)

U.S. Department of Labor Veterans' Employment and Training Service: Plumber (http://doleta.gov)

Vocational Information Center's Masonry Career Guide (http://www.khake.com/page24.html)

What Does an Electrician Do? (http://www.whatdotheydo.com/electric.htm)

FOR FURTHER READING

CARPENTER BOOKS

Dekorne, Clayton. *Trim Carpentry and Built-Ins*. Newtown, CT: Taunton Press, 2002.

Fine Homebuilding. *Finish Carpentry* (For Pros by Pros Series). Newtown, CT: Taunton Press, 2003.

Hamilton, Gene, and Katie Hamilton. *Carpentry for Dummies*. Foster City, CA: IDG Books World Wide, 1999.

Haun, Larry. *Carpentry* (Homebuilding Basics). Newtown, CT: Taunton Press, 1999.

Lewis, Gaspar, and Floyd Vogt. *Carpentry*. Clifton Park, NY: Delmar Learning, 2001.

United States Army Corps of Engineers. Max Fogiel, Ph.D., director. *Basic Carpentry*. Piscataway, NJ: Research and Education Association, 2003.

ELECTRICIAN BOOKS

Black & Decker Home Improvement Library. *Basic Wiring & Electrical Repairs*. Minnetonka, MN: Cowles Creative Publishing Inc., 1990.

Cauldwell, Rex. *Wiring a House*. Newtown, CT: Taunton Press, 1998.

Croft, Terrell, and Wilford I. Summers. *American Electricians' Handbook*. New York: McGraw-Hill, 2002.

Gerrish, Howard H., William E. Dugger Jr., and Kenneth P. DeLucca. *Electricity*. Tinley Park, IL: Goodheart-Wilcox Co., 2004.

Gibilsco, Stan. *Teach Yourself Electricity and Electronics*. New York: McGraw-Hill, 2002.

The Home Depot. *Wiring 1-2-3*. Des Moines, IA: Meredith Books, 2000.

Miller, Charles. *Illustrated Guide to the National Electrical Code*. Clifton Park, NY: Thompson/ Delmar Learning, 2002.

Miller, Charles R. *NEC 2002 Pocket Guide to Electrical Installations*. Quincy, MA: NFPA, 2001.

Miller, Rex. *Electrician's Pocket Manual*. New York: McGraw-Hill, 2000.

Morrison, Ralph. *Electricity: A Self-Teaching Guide*. Hoboken, NJ: John Wiley & Sons, Inc., 2003.

Mullin, Ray C. *House Wiring with the National Electrical Code*. Albany, NY: Delmar, 1999.

National Fire Protection Association, Inc. *NEC 2002 Code (National Electrical Code)*. Quincy, MA: National Fire Protection Association, Inc., 2002.

Rosenberg, Paul. *Questions and Answers for Electrician's Examinations*. Indianapolis, IN: Wiley Publishing, Inc., 2004.

Sorge, Harry W. *Residential Wiring: Based on the 2002 National Electrical Code*. Clifton Park, NY: Delmar Learning, 2003.

Traister, John E. *Electrician's Exam Preparation Guide*. Carlsbad, CA: Craftsman Book Company, 2002.

Tuck, Gary, and David Tuck. *Electricians Instant Answers*. New York: McGraw-Hill, 2004.

United States Naval Personnel. Max Fogiel, Ph.D., director. *Basic Electricity*. Piscataway, NJ: Research and Education Association, 2003.

United States Navy Bureau of United States Naval Personnel. *Basic Electronics*. New York: Dover Publications, 1973.

Wagner, Willis H., and Howard Bud Smith. *Modern Carpentry*. Tinley Park, IL: Goodheart-Wilcox Co., 2003.

MASON BOOKS

Beall, Christine. *Masonry: Design, Build, Maintain.* Upper Saddle River, NJ: Creative Homeowner, 2002.

Black & Decker. *The Complete Guide to Home Masonry.* Chanhassen, MN: Creative Publishing, 2000.

Cory, Steve. *Complete Masonry.* Menlo Park, CA: Sunset Books, 2004.

Jaffe, Rochelle C. *Masonry Instant Answers.* New York: McGraw-Hill, 2004.

Kreh, Dick. *Building with Masonry: Brick, Block & Concrete.* Newtown, CT: Taunton Press, 1998.

PLUMBER BOOKS

Blankenbaker, E. Keith. *Modern Plumbing.* Tinley Park, IL: Goodheart-Wilcox Co., 1997.

Fala, Mario J. *Residential Plumbing Inspector's Manual.* Cleveland, OH: American Society of Sanitary Engineering, 1999.

Guest, J. Russell, Bartholomew D'Arcangelo, and Benedict D'Arcangelo. *Blueprint Reading for Plumbers: Residential and Commercial/Book and Blueprints.* Fifth edition. Clifton Park, NY: Delmar Learning, 1989.

Massey, Howard C. *Plumber's Exam Preparation Guide.* Carlsbad, CA: Craftsman Book Company, 2002.

Massey, Howard C. *Plumber's Handbook.* Carlsbad, CA: Craftsman Book Company, 2002.

Owenby, Charles H., and E. Keith Blankenbaker. *Modern Plumbing* (Workbook). Tinley Park, IL: Goodheart-Wilcox Co., 2000.

Smith, Lee, Benedict D'Arcangelo, and J. Russel Guest. *Mathematics for Plumbers and Pipefitters.* Sixth edition. Clifton Park, NY: Delmar Learning, 2004.

Stanley Books. *Complete Plumbing.* Des Moines, IA: Meredith Books, 2003.

Woodson, R. Dodge. *Plumbing Instant Answers.* New York: McGraw-Hill, 2004.

TILER BOOKS

Barrett, Jim, and Jerry Germer. *Ceramic Tile: Selecting, Installing, Maintaining.* Upper Saddle River, NJ: Creative Homeowner, 2001.

Byrne, Michael. *Setting Tile* (Fine Homebuilding). Newtown, CT: Taunton Press, 1995.

Cory, Steve. *Complete Tile.* Menlo Park, CA: Sunset Books, 2002.

Herbers, Jill, and Roy Wright, photographer. *Tile.* New York: Artisan Sales, 2002.

The Home Depot. *Tiling 1-2-3: Floors, Walls, Countertops, Fireplaces, Decorating Ideas, Custom Design.* Des Moines, IA: Meredith Books, 2001.

Nikitas, Matt. *Grand Finishes for Tile: Home Installation Projects 101.* Torrance, CA: Griffin Trade Paperback, 2001.

Stanley Books. *Basic Tiling: Pro Tips and Simple Tests.* Des Moines, IA: Meredith Books, 2002.

Sunset Staff. *Ideas for Great Tile.* Menlo Park, CA: Sunset Books, 1998.

OTHER HELPFUL BOOKS

Allen, Edward, and Rob Thallon. *Fundamentals of Residential Construction.* New York: John Wiley & Sons, 2002.

Block, Jay A., and Michael Betrus. *101 Best Tech Resumes.* New York: McGraw-Hill, 2003.

Enelow, Wendy S. *Best Resumes for People Without a Four-Year Degree.* Manassas Park, VA: Impact Publications, 2004.

Spencer, Barbara, ed. *Big Book of Jobs 2003–2004*. New York: McGraw-Hill/Contemporary Books, 2002.

Sumichrast, Michael. *Opportunities in Building Construction Trades* (VGM Opportunities Series). Lincolnwood, IL: VGM Career Horizons, 1998.

BIBLIOGRAPHY

Bureau of Labor Statistics, U.S. Department of Labor. *Occupational Outlook Handbook, 2002–03 Edition: Carpenters.* Retrieved June 15, 2004 (http://www.bls.gov/oco/ocos202.htm).

Electricity Online "Electricity: Detailed Timeline." Retrieved August 26, 2004 (http://library.thinkquest.org/28032/cgi-bin/psparse.cgi?src = history07).

Mahieur, Louis J. *The Plumber's Toolbox Manual* (Arco Books). New York: Macmillan General Reference, 1989.

Massey, Howard C. *Plumber's Exam Preparation Guide.* Carlsbad, CA: Craftsman Book Company, 2002.

Nycareerzone.org. "Brickmasons and Blockmasons: An Occupation in Engineering and Technologies." Retrieved August 26, 2004 (http://www.nycareerzone.org/graphic/profile.jsp;jsessionid = 786951098982334991?onetsoc = 47-2021.00).

Phifer, Paul. *Great Careers in 2 Years: The Associate Degree Option.* New York: Ferguson/Facts on File, 2003.

Salary.com. "Job Valuation Report for Plumber III." Retrieved August 26, 2004 (http://secure.salary.com/jobvaluationreport/docs/jobvaluationreport/joblisthtmls/jvrjob_SC16000006.html).

Simonson, Ken. "Construction Employment Climbs in December; Broader Economy Appears to Slow," *Plumbing and Mechanical Magazine*, January 2004.

Traister, John E. *Electrician's Exam Preparation Guide.* Carlsbad, CA: Craftsman Book Company, 2002.

The United States Department of Labor. *Occupational Outlook Handbook 2002-2003.* Chicago: VGM Career Books, 2002.

INTERVIEWS

Interview via e-mail with Jacob Fisher, January 27, 2004.

Interview via e-mail with Eddy Wright, February 3, 2004.

Interview via e-mail with Scott McDanel, February 18, 2004.

Interview via e-mail with Will Munroe, February 21, 2004.

Interview via telephone with Randy Chalfant, March 4, 2004.

Interview with Chris Sainz, March 7, 2004.

Interview via telephone with Jarrett Tatge, March 8, 2004.

Interview via telephone with Terry Mulligan, March 11, 2004.

INDEX

ACKNOWLEDGMENTS

I would like to thank Linda Chalfant Coy, Michele Hammer Ottenfeld, Dawn Malone, Cathy Carnevale Wright, Kerstain McWhorter, Donna Schmitz, Aime Johnson, Jim O'Connor, April Biggs, and Kathy Valdez-Hardy for putting me in touch with so many wonderful tradesmen.

My thanks also to Jacob Fisher, Randy Chalfant, Will Munroe, Eddy Wright, Scott McDanel, Chris Sainz, Jarrett Tatge, and Terry Mulligan for taking time from their busy schedules to let me interview them for this book.

My gratitude to Tina P. Schwartz, Kathy Christopher French, Meredith Schaab, Debbie Price, K. F. Turtletaub, and Darwin R. Apel for their stories about why these tradesmen are so vital.

And special thanks AGAIN to Mindy S. Apel, who so willingly assisted with the grunt work without grunting even once. You all helped make this book what it is! Thank you!

ABOUT THE AUTHOR

Melanie Ann Apel has a bachelor's degree in theater arts from Bradley University and another in respiratory care from National-Louis University. She has written more than forty nonfiction books for children and young adults. In addition, she has written and compiled photos for a pictorial history of her Chicago neighborhood, entitled *Lincoln Park, Chicago*. Apel and her husband have two sons.